ReadyGEN
Collection 5

ISBN-13: 978-0-328-85285-7
ISBN-10: 0-328-85285-6
19 2022

Table of Contents

Unit 3 Understanding the Universe

Unit 4 Exploring New Worlds

Acknowledgments

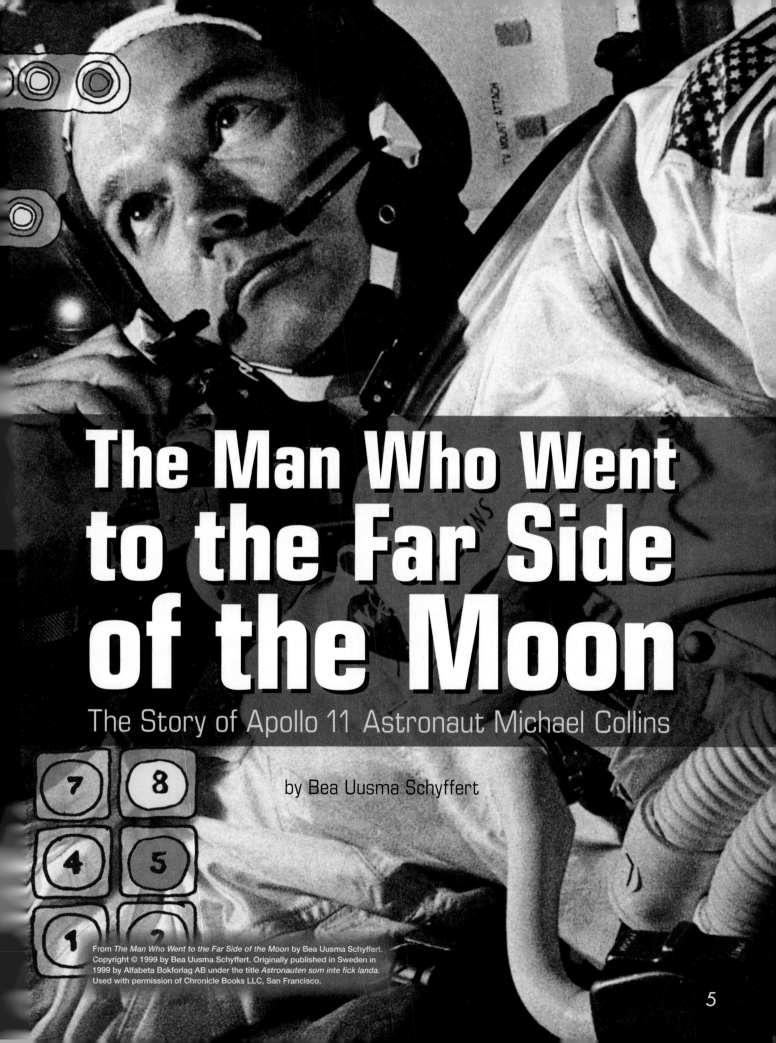

The Man Who Went to the Far Side of the Moon

The Story of Apollo 11 Astronaut Michael Collins

by Bea Uusma Schyffert

On July 16, 1969, the United States launched the *Saturn 5* rocket into space. Aboard this spacecraft, the largest rocket ever built, were three men: astronauts Michael Collins, Buzz Aldrin, and Neil Armstrong. Their mission: to be the first to land on the moon. One of these men would not land on the moon, however. That man, Michael Collins, would circle the moon in the command module while Buzz Aldrin and Neil Armstrong landed the lunar module, *Eagle*, and explored the moon's surface.

It is July 20, 1969. A Sunday. It's four minutes to ten in the morning. It is –250°F (–180°C) in the shade and +250°F (+120°C) in the sun at the Sea of Tranquility, where Neil and Buzz have landed the *Eagle*. They are 242,000 miles (390,000 kilometers) from Launch Pad 39A at Kennedy Space Center in Florida.

In the earliest versions of the checklists, Buzz Aldrin would be the first man to step down onto the moon. But the lunar module hatch opens inward to the right, and Buzz, who stood right behind it, had difficulty climbing out. When the astronauts tried to switch places during practice, they damaged the cramped cabin. A few months before the launch, it was decided that Neil should go first. He crawls backward through a tiny hatch near the floor. As he looks toward the horizon, he can see that they have landed on a sphere: the horizon is a little bent since the moon is so small. His arms are covered with goose bumps. There is no air. No sound. No life. No footprints.

Wait: now there is one.

Neil Armstrong is the first man on the moon.

...I'M GOING TO STEP OFF THE LM NOW...

When you stand on the moon, you can cover the entire Earth with your hand.

242,000 miles (390,000 kilometers) from home, trapped inside a small vessel, two men are taking snapshots of each other.

Neil Armstrong's picture of Buzz Aldrin

Buzz Aldrin's picture of Neil Armstrong

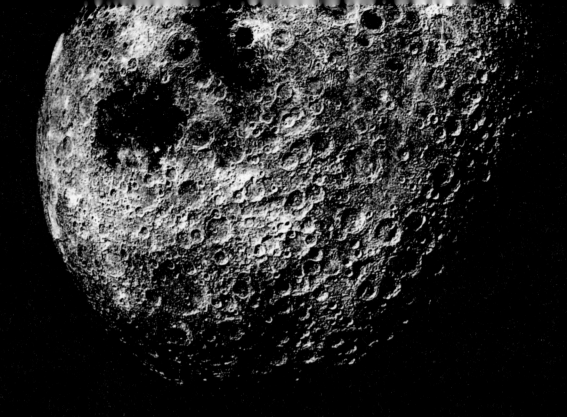

Neil and Buzz stay on the moon for 21 hours and 36 minutes, but only a little more than 2 hours of that time is spent outside the lunar module. They perform three minor experiments and load two aluminum suitcases with 48 pounds (22 kilograms) of moon dust and rocks.

The three minor experiments:
    To measure solar particles
    To measure the exact distance to Earth
    To measure moonquakes and meteoritic impact

The major experiment:
    To land on the moon

When they have climbed back into the lunar module and shut the hatch, they take their helmets off. They look at each other because they both sense a strong smell. Neil thinks it smells like wet ashes. Buzz says it smells like spent gunpowder. It is the moon. The moon has a smell.

Six hundred million people in 47 countries are watching the blurred TV transmission of the lunar landing. There is one person who has no chance of catching Neil and Buzz on TV. He is traveling at a height of 70 miles (110 kilometers) above the far side of the moon. All he can see is darkness and stars outside his window.

In case something unexpected should happen, the astronauts never bounce farther than 200 feet (60 meters) from the landing site.

Michael Collins has 28 hours to go, alone in the capsule. He has trained for so long. He has traveled so far. He is so close now and still he can't land on the moon. They did not choose him.

He was going for 99 percent of the trip and that was good enough for him, he has replied when people have asked. But he knew he didn't have the best seat on *Columbia*.

He thinks to himself that he never really got to know the astronauts who are now on the moon. Neil and Buzz trained together for many months in the lunar module simulator. Michael trained by himself in the capsule.

Once every two hours *Columbia* passes over the landing site. Michael Collins tries to locate the *Eagle*. He can't see it. He only sees crater after crater, cast with sharp shadows from the sun.

apollo 11, this is houston, we're three minutes away from loss of signal over

Every other hour, all radio communication with Earth is lost as the spacecraft skims over the far side of the moon. When Neil and Buzz are on the moon's surface, Michael Collins has to do three people's jobs. He has to make 850 computer commands. He has been taught just *how* to push the buttons—hard, right in the center, and to hold them pushed for a little over a second. They must be pushed in the right order, one after the other: VERB-88-ENTER. VERB-87-ENTER. If he loses track on the far side of the moon, there is no one to ask.

Michael turns up the light in the command module. It's almost cozy. He is used to flying alone. He has flown airplanes by himself for almost 20 years. He has even practiced how he should return home by himself if something should happen to Neil and Buzz down on the moon.

It's quiet in the capsule on the dark side of the moon. The only noises are the fans humming and a faint crackling from the radio. Michael Collins prepares his dinner. Looks out the windows. Every 120th minute he sees the Earth rise at the horizon.

MICHAEL COLLINS'S FOOD PACK ON THE FOURTH DAY OF THE TRIP

BREAKFAST:

FROSTED FLAKES
(FREEZE-DRIED)

4 PEANUT CUBES
(BITE-SIZED)

COCOA (POWDER)

ORANGE AND
GRAPEFRUIT DRINK
(POWDER)

CANADIAN BACON
AND APPLESAUCE
(FREEZE-DRIED)

LUNCH:

SHRIMP COCKTAIL
(FREEZE-DRIED)

HAM AND POTATOES
(WET-PACK)

FRUIT COCKTAIL
(FREEZE-DRIED)

4 DATE FRUITCAKE
CUBES (BITE-SIZED)

GRAPEFRUIT DRINK
(POWDER)

DINNER:

BEEF STEW
(SPOON-BOWL)

4 COCONUT CUBES
(BITE-SIZED)

BANANA PUDDING
(POWDER)

GRAPE PUNCH (POWDER)

ALL THE FOOD IS VACUUM PACKED AND MARKED WITH LABELS, SINCE IT IS DIFFICULT TO TELL
WHAT EACH ITEM IS SUPPOSED TO BE. THE TRICKY THING ABOUT EATING IN WEIGHTLESSNESS IS
MOVING THE FOOD FROM THE PACKAGE TO THE MOUTH, WITHOUT LETTING IT FLOAT AWAY. THE
ASTRONAUTS EAT:

FREEZE-DRIED AND POWDERED FOOD:

THEY INJECT COLD OR HOT
WATER INTO THE PACKAGE
WITH A SPECIAL WATER GUN,
SQUEEZE THE PACKAGE FOR
ABOUT THREE MINUTES,
THEN CUT OFF A CORNER
AND SQUEEZE THE PASTE
INTO THEIR MOUTHS.

WET-PACKED FOOD:

THEY SUCK THE READY-MIXED
WET-PACK FOOD, COLD,
STRAIGHT OUT OF
THE PACKAGE.

SPOON-BOWL FOOD:

THEY INJECT COLD OR HOT
WATER WITH THE WATER GUN
AND SQUEEZE THE PACKAGE
A LITTLE BEFORE THEY OPEN
THE TOP. SPOON-BOWL FOOD
IS EATEN WITH A SPOON. IT
IS SO STICKY THAT IT EITHER
STAYS IN THE PACKAGE OR
CLINGS TO THE SPOON.

It is July 24, 1969. A Thursday. Ever since they left the moon, the astronauts have been eager to get back home. After 8 days, 3 hours, and 18 minutes in *Columbia* without washing, the entire body itches. It is hard to breathe in the spacecraft now. It smells like wet dogs and rotten swamp. Michael Collins has flown *Columbia* during reentry into the Earth's atmosphere. For 14 minutes, the astronauts have been pushed down into their seats. They have weighed seven times their weight on Earth. Now the capsule has splashed down in the ocean near Hawaii.

No one knows if the astronauts have been exposed to dangerous lunar germs that could potentially wipe out the human race. Because of this they are sent straight to a quarantine facility: a silver-colored mobile home. Inside, the astronauts write reports about their trip. Michael beats Neil in cards. As they sit there, bored as can be, they begin to understand just what they have experienced. During the trip itself they were so focused on their job that they didn't have time to think about what they have actually done. Everyone on Earth gathered together because of the moon landing. But the astronauts themselves have been far, far away.

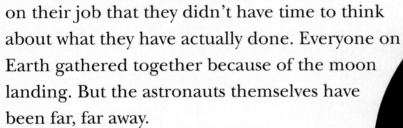
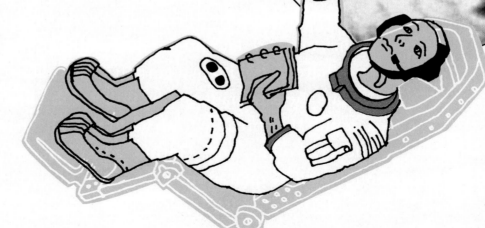

apollo 11, this is houston do you copy?

As they watch a taped recording of the moon landing, Buzz suddenly turns to Neil and says: "Neil, we missed the whole thing!"

In the past, Michael Collins never really cared about the machines he has flown, but this time it's different. On the second night of quarantine, he climbs back into *Columbia* and takes a seat. Then he leans over and scribbles a message in ballpoint pen on the capsule wall, in the tiniest handwriting imaginable:

> *Spacecraft 107—alias Apollo 11—alias Columbia*
> *The best ship to come down the line*
> *God bless her*
> *Michael Collins, CMP*

To find out if the astronauts are carrying deadly germs, mice are let into the quarantine trailer. The mice have grown up in a germ-free laboratory. After 17 days the astronauts are let out. For the first time in a month they breathe fresh air. If the mice had died, Michael Collins, Buzz Aldrin, and Neil Armstrong might still be quarantined.

LEFT ON THE MOON

SINCE *APOLLO 11*, THERE HAVE BEEN FIVE OTHER LUNAR MODULES ON THE MOON. THE LAST ONE LANDED IN 1972. EVERYTHING THE ASTRONAUTS LEFT BEHIND STAYS EXACTLY LIKE IT WAS WHEN IT WAS FIRST PUT THERE. THERE IS NO RUST. THERE IS NO WEAR AND TEAR. IN THE GRAY MOON DUST LIE THE TRACES OF SIX APOLLO MISSIONS:

2 GOLF BALLS HIT BY ASTRONAUT ALAN SHEPARD (*APOLLO 14*)	3 MOON BUGGIES (FROM *APOLLO 15, 16,* AND *17*)	A SCULPTURE OF A FALLEN ASTRONAUT, IN MEMORY OF ALL THOSE WHO HAVE DIED IN THE EFFORTS TO REACH THE MOON
TO SAVE ON WEIGHT, THE ASTRONAUTS LEFT EVERYTHING THEY DIDN'T NEED BEFORE TAKING OFF IN THE LUNAR MODULE: SCIENTIFIC EXPERIMENTS TV CAMERAS AND CABLES HASSELBLAD CAMERAS EMPTY FOOD PACKAGES	MEMENTOS AND HONORARY OBJECTS: PLAQUES MEDALLIONS ASTRONAUT BADGES CRUCIFIXES A GOLD OLIVE BRANCH A COMPUTER DISC THE SIZE OF A SILVER DOLLAR WITH PEACEFUL GREETINGS FROM PRESIDENTS AND PRIME MINISTERS OF 73 COUNTRIES	ONE RED BIBLE
		6 AMERICAN FLAGS
PARTS OF THE SPACESUITS: BACKPACK, BOOTS		UNVERIFIED: LAS BRISAS HOTEL IN ACAPULCO, MEXICO, INSISTS THAT THE *APOLLO 11* ASTRONAUTS PLACED A PINK FLAG FROM THE HOTEL ON THE MOON IN GRATITUDE FOR THEIR COMPLIMENTARY STAY.
6 LUNAR MODULES		

OVER FOUR HUNDRED SIXTY THOUSAND PEOPLE WORKED ON THE APOLLO PROJECT. THEY GOT 12 ASTRONAUTS TO THE MOON. ALTOGETHER, THE APOLLO ASTRONAUTS BROUGHT 840 POUNDS (380 KILOGRAMS) OF MOON MATERIAL BACK TO EARTH. ON THE MOON THERE ARE FOOTPRINTS FROM 12 PEOPLE, TRACES THAT WILL NEVER BE SWEPT AWAY BY ANY WIND.

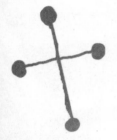

When Michael Collins returned from the moon, he made a decision to never travel again. He wanted to spend the rest of his life fishing, bringing up his children, taking care of his dogs, and sitting on the porch with his wife.

Sometimes, when he's talking to other people, the thought strikes him: *I have been to places and done things that no one can ever imagine. I will never be able to explain what it was like. I carry it inside, like a treasure.*

At night, Michael Collins tends to the roses in his garden at the back of his house. The soil smells good. The wind feels warm and humid against his face. He looks up at the yellow disk in the sky and thinks to himself: *I have been there. It was beautiful, but compared to Earth it was nothing.*

He never wants to go back to the moon.

16

We're lucky to have
this planet. I know.

Mayday on Moon of Jupiter

by Stacia Deutsch

"Mayday! Mayday! Mayday!"

Justin Marsen pulled back on the steering column with his right hand while hammering on the autopilot controller with his left.

"We're going down," Justin's copilot and twin sister Alicia said in a calm, matter-of-fact voice.

"Do something!!" he shouted frantically, giving the panel a punch that cracked the touch screen display.

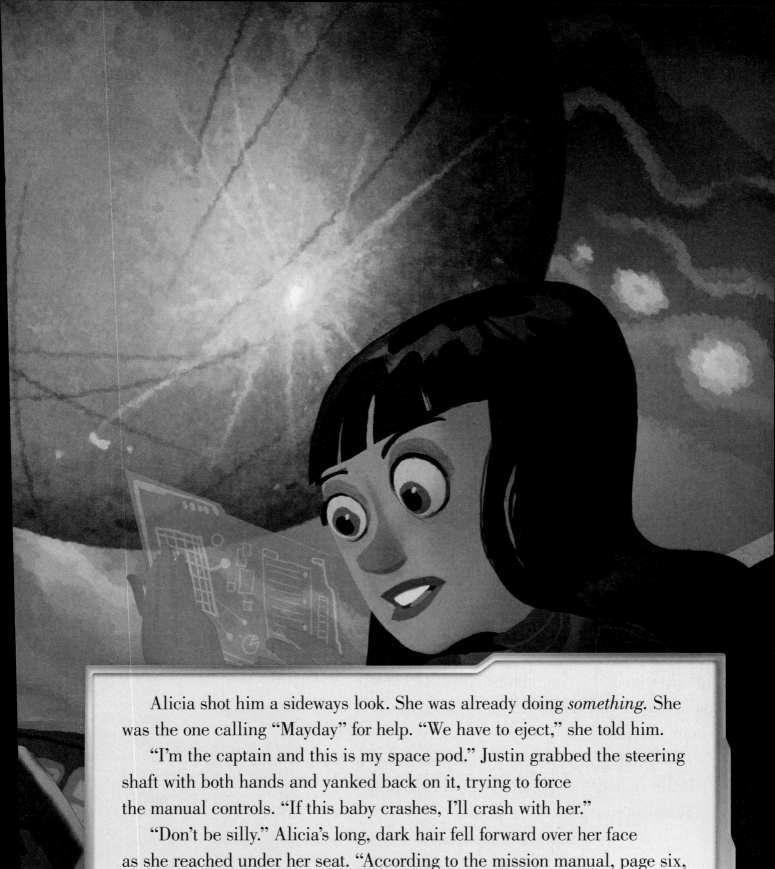

Alicia shot him a sideways look. She was already doing *something*. She was the one calling "Mayday" for help. "We have to eject," she told him.

"I'm the captain and this is my space pod." Justin grabbed the steering shaft with both hands and yanked back on it, trying to force the manual controls. "If this baby crashes, I'll crash with her."

"Don't be silly." Alicia's long, dark hair fell forward over her face as she reached under her seat. "According to the mission manual, page six, paragraph two, there's only one thing to do in a situation like this. . . ." She glared at her brother, and then twisted a glowing red knob.

The next thing Justin knew, he was lying on the ground, battered and bruised. His back hurt. He had a headache. And he was freezing cold.

Justin struggled to stand up only to discover he was wearing a special protective crash suit, complete with a heavy oxygenated helmet. That explained the headache. In an emergency, the suit emerged from the pod's seat back and wrapped itself gently around the flyer. The helmet, however, dropped like lead from the ceiling.

He groaned and shook off the pain radiating from the top of his skull.

The helmet visor made it difficult to judge exactly where he had crash-landed. There was a reflection in the mask that showed his own dark brown eyes staring back at him.

Justin stood up. "Oof!" He slipped and immediately crashed back down onto the hard, firm ground.

Leaning up on an elbow, Justin looked around. Ice, smooth and slick like a skating rink, stretched out in every direction. Moving slowly, Justin managed to stand again and took a cautious step forward.

"Alicia?" he called. It was bad enough that he had crash-landed on an unfamiliar planet. Worse that he had dragged his sister into this mess. "Alicia! Where are you?!"

The freezing wind made him shiver.

Justin sighed. For months, he had begged his parents to let him go on this mission. They argued that he was too young. He argued that he could handle it. Finally, they agreed—as long as Alicia went along too.

She didn't want to go. She didn't like leaving Earth. But Justin couldn't go without her, so he did everything he could think of to get her in the pod. He folded her laundry and cleaned her room. He even promised he would do her chores for a year.

"Alicia, where are you?" Justin surveyed the ice-crusted planet. The land around him was dotted with frozen hills and jagged cliff faces. "Alicia?" There was no reply. "Alicia!!"

"Justin?" Her voice came from behind the smoldering wreckage of the pod. "Over here."

The cabin of the ship was lying on its side and smelled like burning rubber. A gaping hole in the side of the fuselage revealed scattered equipment and melted wiring.

Alicia was sitting on a hunk of severed aluminum holding the charred remains of the mission manual. "Page eight, paragraph three," she read, "the crew may not stray from the ship."

"Alicia!" Justin slipped and stumbled his way to her and after skidding to a stop, gave her a hug.

"You promised nothing bad would happen." She didn't hug him back. "You *never* keep your promises." Arms pinned to her sides, she said, "I bet you were never really going to do my chores at all."

Justin didn't reply. He moved clumsily away, staring down at the ice.

Alicia wrapped her arms around herself and asked in a weak voice, "Can you get us home?"

Guilt settled in his chest as Justin studied the space pod. He could fix most anything. But without the right parts, there was no way to repair the damage. The pod was ruined. He told her the truth. "No."

Justin stared out towards the skyline. He could see the Jovian rings of Jupiter glowing in the distance. Several of Jupiter's moons glinted with reflected light from the sun. "This isn't Jupiter, is it?" he asked, though the answer was obvious.

Alicia pointed to a massive planet in the distance. "We shot past it."

"Must have happened after the iron-core reactor dried out." Justin wrung his gloved hands together. "Looks like the back-up power booster gave one last boost before it died." He looked at the ship. "Do you think Mom and Dad heard the 'Mayday'?"

Alicia shrugged. "I doubt it."

Justin nodded. "Well, then, what does the manual say to do now?"

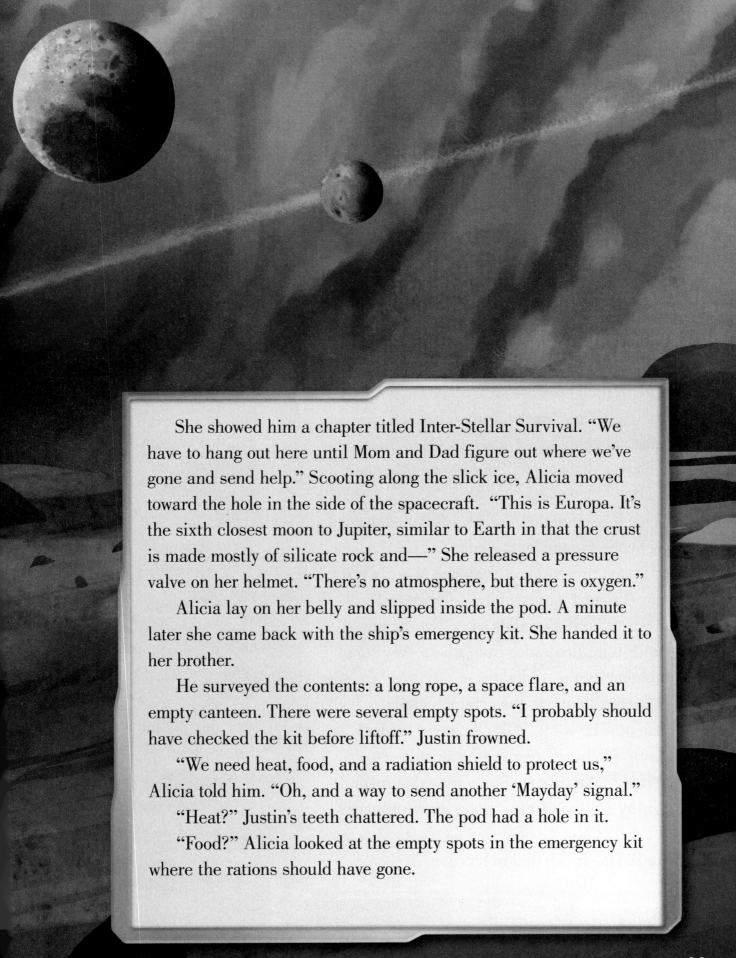

She showed him a chapter titled Inter-Stellar Survival. "We have to hang out here until Mom and Dad figure out where we've gone and send help." Scooting along the slick ice, Alicia moved toward the hole in the side of the spacecraft. "This is Europa. It's the sixth closest moon to Jupiter, similar to Earth in that the crust is made mostly of silicate rock and—" She released a pressure valve on her helmet. "There's no atmosphere, but there is oxygen."

Alicia lay on her belly and slipped inside the pod. A minute later she came back with the ship's emergency kit. She handed it to her brother.

He surveyed the contents: a long rope, a space flare, and an empty canteen. There were several empty spots. "I probably should have checked the kit before liftoff." Justin frowned.

"We need heat, food, and a radiation shield to protect us," Alicia told him. "Oh, and a way to send another 'Mayday' signal."

"Heat?" Justin's teeth chattered. The pod had a hole in it.

"Food?" Alicia looked at the empty spots in the emergency kit where the rations should have gone.

"No." Justin shook his head.

"Communications?" she asked.

He shook his head again. There was no point in asking about the radiation shield.

With a frustrated sigh, Alicia began to flip through the manual as if the answer to their problem was hidden somewhere in the pages. "Europa is a little bigger than our own moon. It'll rotate around to this spot in Jupiter's orbit in three and a half days," she said. "The most important thing is the shield. In an hour, the radiation will increase. Without protection, we'll die."

She turned the manual so he could see a picture in the appendix.

"Eww. Gross." Justin turned his head away. He was not going to let *that* happen to them. "An hour . . ." There had to be something he could do.

The *Marsen 8 Mission* consisted of eight ships headed to the eight planets of Earth's solar system in search of evidence of early life forms. The next closest ship had gone to Mars. That was 93 million miles away. Saturn was about 406 million miles from where they stood at this time in the orbital cycle.

"Even if I can get the communication system up," he said, "it'll take a pod too long to get here. We have to repair the shield."

"How?" Alicia gave him a look that made the guilty feeling in Justin's gut grow stronger.

"I don't know." There was no choice. It was life or death. Justin had to try.

Using all his strength, he peeled off a broken panel on the outside of the space pod. The heart of the ship was completely fried. The wiring was cinder. The components black with ash. He tossed the trashed parts aside and focused on finding the one thing he might be able to use.

"Good news." The casing for the iron-fusion reactor was completely intact. Justin tugged the device away from the wiring and stepped back from the ship.

The baseball-sized fusion reactor was Justin's own invention. While other ships used cold fusion, Justin had replaced his reactor with one that used iron at the core and could fuse most any other material—as long as there was water buffering the compounds, the reactor could provide unlimited energy. He was planning to tell his parents all about it after the mission was a success.

Unfortunately, halfway to Jupiter, the water evaporated. Justin hadn't accounted for the need to refill.

"If we can find water, I can get the pod's radiation shields up and running and generate enough power to start up the communications system," Justin told Alicia. "I can even get us heat."

"Let's melt some of this ice," Alicia suggested. She took the flare from the emergency kit and cracked it. The light glowed green. "Chemiluminesence," she said, pinching her lips. "No sparks."

Suddenly, a frozen wind blew with such force that it knocked Justin backwards. "WHOA!" He fell on the ice, and the small fusion reactor slipped from his hand and rolled away. He shouted to Alicia, "Get the orb!"

"We can't leave the ship!" Alicia cried as Justin threw himself forward and slid across the moon's rough surface. "Paragraph—"

"Forget the manual!" Justin bumped over a lumpy part of the frozen moon surface that had dark brown crisscrossed lines embedded in the ice. "We need that reactor!"

Quickly glancing over his shoulder, he could see Alicia's look of doubt as she set down the booklet. She took a running leap and belly-flopped onto the ice, flying forward with such speed that she passed Justin by.

"Way to go, Alicia!"

One second Alicia was in front of him, the next she had disappeared from the moon's surface. "AHHHH!"

"Alicia!" Justin dragged his feet and stopped. Alicia was nowhere in view. He'd lost her again . . . "Alicia?"

"I found the reactor," she said. Her voice echoed softly and far away.

Justin moved to the edge of a deep crack. The reactor was no longer his main concern. "Are you hurt?" Alicia was so far down the crevasse that he could barely see the top of her helmet.

"I'm okay," her voice echoed.

"Tie this around your waist." Justin dropped the emergency rope down to her.

"Ready," she said. Then, "No. Wait. Send down the canteen first."

"Why?" he asked. "It's empty."

"Trust me," Alicia told him.

Justin passed her the canteen and then walked back to the ship. He tied his end of the rope around the heaviest piece of twisted metal.

Justin and Alicia worked together to pull her out of the crevasse.

"Here." She handed him the canteen.

"What is it?" He twisted off the lid and smelled the contents. "Water?" Then cheered, "Water!" Justin grinned. "As long as we have water, we can stay as long as we need to." He filled the iron-fusion reactor. It immediately began to glow a healthy orange. He repaired the radiation shield while Alicia contacted their parents.

Help was on the way.

"While we're hanging out, I think I'll read the mission manual," Justin said, picking up the thick booklet. "Page one. Paragraph one."

"You don't need to read it." Alicia gave her brother a crushing hug. "I'll come along on your next voyage and tell you what you need to know." Very excited, she explained, "You did a good job, Justin. This mission was a huge success."

"It was?" Justin asked, wrinkling his eyebrows. He glanced at Jupiter—the planet where they should have landed. "It feels like a failure."

"Do you know what we found?" Alicia laughed at Justin's blank stare. "We found water. That's the first sign of potential life." She shook the canteen. "Under the sea on Earth, way down by the core, plants and animals can grow. Maybe that's happening here too!"

"Sounds like there's a lot more exploring to be done on Europa," Justin agreed.

"I can't wait." Alicia leaned back and watched the stars twinkle.

"It'll be an adventure." Justin looked at his sister and smiled. "I promise."

A Black Hole Is NOT a Hole

Then what is it?

by Carolyn Cinami DeCristofano

illustrated by Michael Carroll

A black hole is NOT a hole—
at least not the kind you can
dig in the ground
or poke your finger through.
You can't just walk along
and fall into one.
A black hole isn't a hole
like that.

If a black hole is not a hole,
then what in the universe is it?

Places with Pull

A black hole is a place in space with a powerful pull.

Way out beyond where you are right now, beyond the clouds, beyond the Moon, beyond Pluto, beyond our solar system, space goes on and on. You could travel for trillions of miles and you'd barely get to the closest star. In another few trillion miles you might pass another star. Space is that huge.

Way out there, trillions, quadrillions, and even more *-illions* of miles away, are special places called black holes. These places in space are special because of their powerful pull on other things. A black hole's pull is the strongest pull in the entire universe.

Nothing can out-tug a black hole. No army of tow trucks, no convoy of supersized earth haulers, no fleet of giant rocket engines. Not all of them combined.

A black hole pulls in nearby dust. It pulls in nearby asteroids. It pulls in nearby stars and even nearby starlight. And no light, stars, asteroids, or dust comes out. Not ever.

A black hole is like a giant whirlpool.

Have you ever pulled out a sink stopper and watched water swirl down the drain? Spirals of water flow toward the center. You've made a small whirlpool.

Imagine a bigger whirlpool in a river. Far away, nobody knows it's there. Boats chug and sail along. Schools of fish dart by, following their fishy urges. Closer to the whirlpool, it's a different story.

A fish swimming near the whirlpool's edge feels a gentle tug as the current drags it toward the spinning center. No problem. With a little swish, the fish can speed up, giving itself the oomph to swim away. After putting some distance between itself and the whirlpool, the fish no longer feels the current's inward pull.

But what if the fish drifted farther in?

Closer to the center of the whirlpool, the pull would grow stronger. To escape the whirlpool, the fish would have to swim faster than it had to at the edge. Even closer to the middle, if the fish couldn't go much faster, it would find itself swept all the way in, stuck in the swirl, pulled round and round and round.

A black hole works something like that whirlpool.

Even though a black hole's pull is the strongest in the universe, it's not strong from far away. Galaxies and stardust drifting through space don't get dragged into a distant black hole.

What a drag!

However, near a black hole, gases and dust and stars encounter its tug. Some things may be hurtling by so fast they won't get pulled into the black hole. Other things may not be as swift. They will be drawn in.

Closer and closer, the tugging force gets stronger and stronger. Close enough, the black hole no longer acts like a whirlpool.

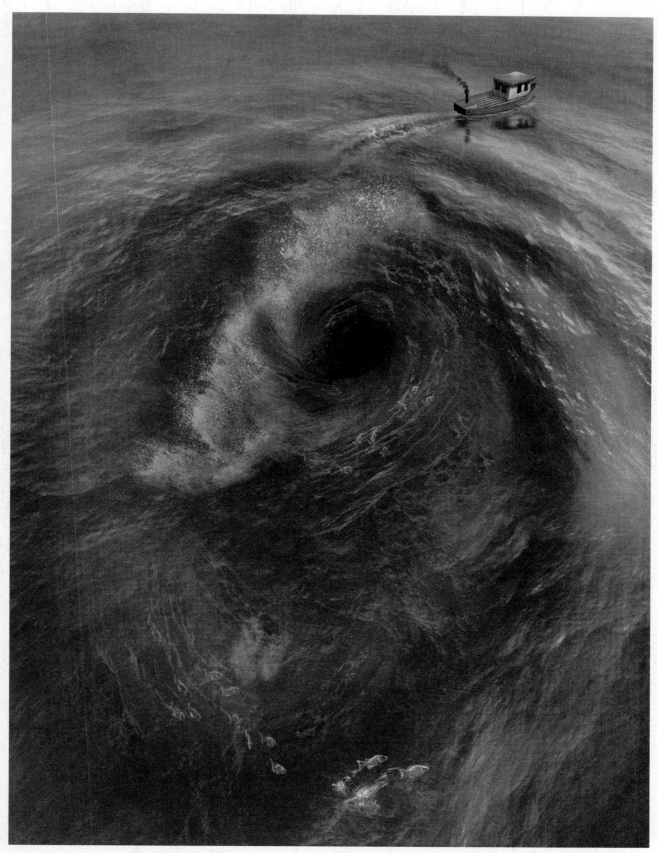

The inward pull of a swirling whirlpool gets stronger near its center. The closer a fish (or anything else) gets to the center, the more speed it needs to get out.

Even though it's like a whirlpool, a black hole is not a whirlpool.

With a whirlpool, there's always a fast-enough fish—or a fast-enough *something*—th[at] [m]ough so quickly it won't be pulled all the wa[y] [to] the center.

Not so with a black hole! Within a ce[rtain] distance the black hole's power is so stron[g] nothing is fast enough to zip away.

This is a black hole's special trait: its supe[r] pulling zone. Outside the zone, there's always the chance that something will zoom past and away. But anything inside this zone stays in the black hole's place in space forever. Nothing else in the universe is so inescapable.

So a black hole is NOT a whirlpool. It just (sort of) acts like one.

There's another difference. In a whirlpool, the swirling current of water draws the fish into the center. But a black hole isn't made of water. Something else drives its pulling power.

Like a fish caught in a whirlpool, colorful, glowing gases swirl toward a black hole. The dark center marks the black hole's super-pulling zone. (Artist's representation)

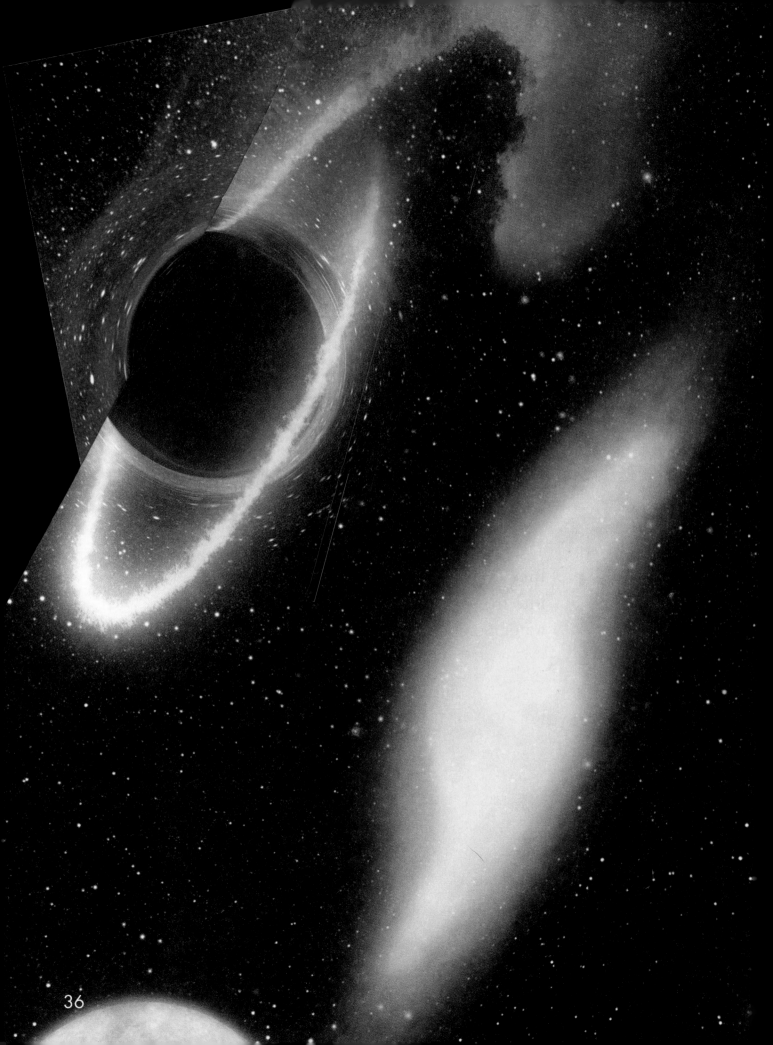

The Pulling Power of a Black Hole

A black hole is an extreme gravity zone.

Gravity is the source of a black hole's super pull.

You deal with gravity every day. You count on it to bring you back to the ground when you jump up. You depend on it when you try to catch a pop fly, knowing the ball will fall down. You expect it to be there, even if you don't think about it much.

People must have always noticed that objects fall, but they didn't know what made this happen. They certainly didn't guess that falling objects had anything to do with the stars, Moon, planets, and Sun—but then one man came along with some new ideas.

Gravity Rules

That man was Isaac Newton. In 1687 he proposed that objects fall to the ground because Earth pulls on them. But his idea reached beyond Earth. He suggested that *all* things pull on each other, even when they are not touching. He considered this pull a force of nature and referred to it as *gravitas*—what we now call gravity.

Just outside a black hole's extreme gravity zone, its gravitation is still remarkable. In this artist's picture, a black hole pulls clouds of gas off a nearby star.

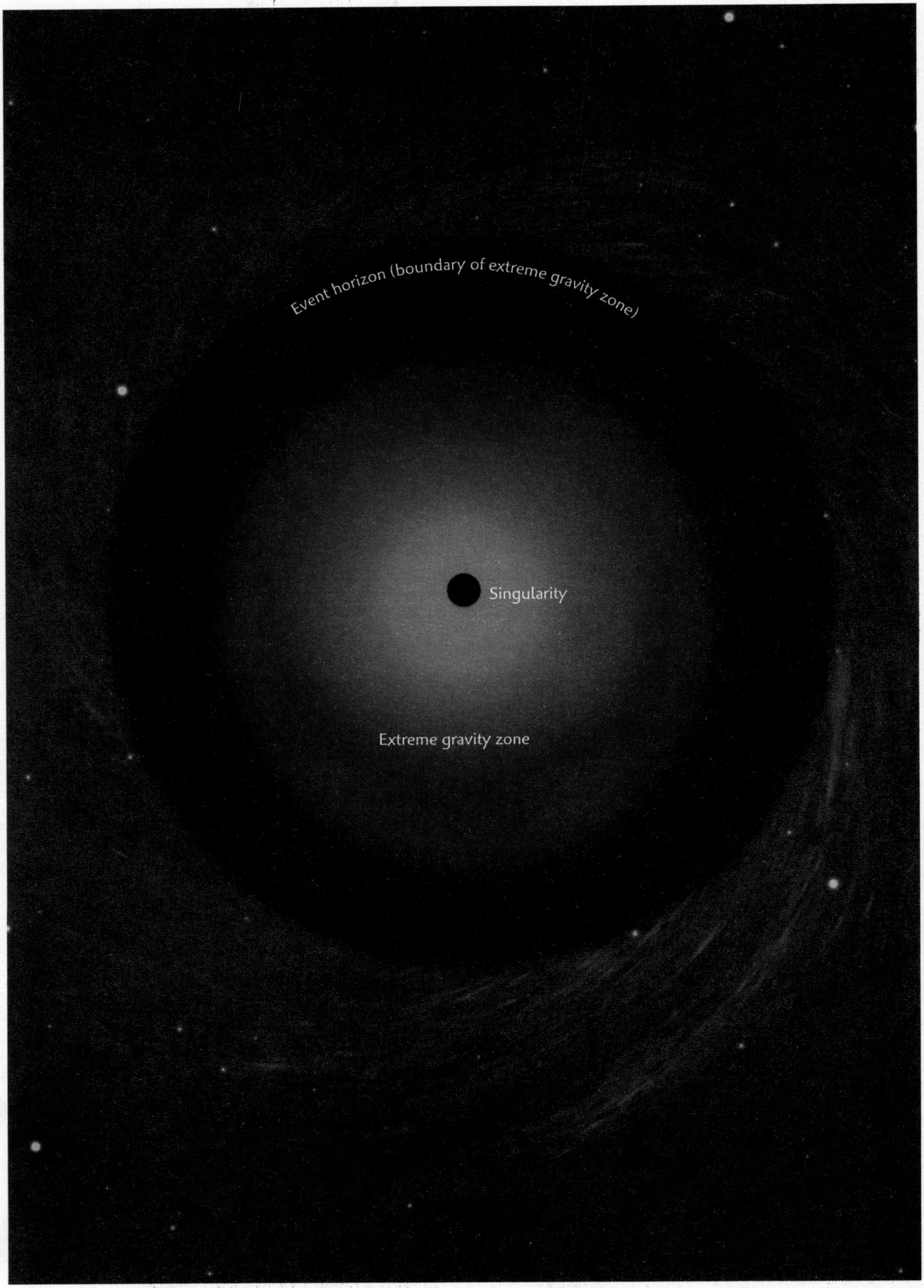

Event horizon (boundary of extreme gravity zone)

Singularity

Extreme gravity zone

An Extreme Case of Gravity

Remember that super-pulling space around a black hole—the one with the strongest pull in the universe? That super pull is the close-up gravitational power of a black hole. Here in this zone, the gravity is so intense that nothing can move fast enough to fly, launch, jump, or zoom away.

Around this extreme zone is a boundary called the event horizon. This boundary acts like a point of no return. Once past it, there's no going back. Only black holes have such extreme gravity zones, and only black holes have event horizons. This is what makes a black hole different from everything else.

But a black hole is more than just a gravity zone—more than just empty space inside an event horizon. A black hole also includes the source of its tremendous gravitation: a massive amount of densely packed matter sitting at its center. The matter is so densely packed that it forms a single point, called a singularity.

Where does this matter come from? How did it get to be so densely packed? And what does it have to do with the beginning of a black hole?

The answers lie in the stars.

This cross-section diagram shows the anatomy of a black hole. At the center is an extremely small, densely packed singularity, super-enlarged for visibility. Surrounding the singularity is an extreme gravity zone, colored red. The outer boundary of this zone is the event horizon. (Diagram not to scale)

An Event What?

Have you ever watched the Sun set? After it sinks below the horizon, Earth blocks your view of it. Even though you know it's still out there in space, you can't see it. Any and all events on the Sun remain invisible to you for as long as it is below the horizon. If the Sun suddenly turned purple, you wouldn't see it happen.

In a similar way, once an object enters the extreme gravity zone of a black hole, the object disappears from view. Even though nothing physically blocks our sight, once the object is beyond the boundary of the zone, we cannot see what happens to it. Events beyond the black hole's "horizon" are invisible to us. Because of this visual effect, scientists named the boundary the *event horizon*.

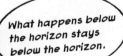

What happens below the horizon stays below the horizon.

Black-Hole Beginnings

The beginning of a black hole can be the end of something else.

Black holes come from stars.

Every star has a beginning, when light first bursts from it. Then it shines on and on, for millions, even billions, of years. But every star comes to an end. And sometimes a star's final moments are an all-out frenzy. After the dust clears, a black hole may be all that's left.

Black hole's first picture

Awww . . .

Star Power

Before a star is a star, it is an enormous cloud of gases. At the start, wisps of gas and drifts of dust collect, their gravity drawing them together. As more stuff gathers, its combined gravitation grows stronger. Eventually the cloud pulls itself into a massive ball of material.

Under the force of its own weight, the gigantic ball presses inward. Deep beneath the surface, the intense pressure squeezes the material, like the powerful grip of a giant hand. The inner material packs together tightly. More matter mounts up on the outside, increasing the pressure on the inside. Soon the pressure in the center is so high, it ignites a booming nuclear reaction. Starlight bursts from the ball of gas. Now blazing, flaring, spewing, and spouting, the new star is a fiery furnace.

Sparking a Star

A star's fiery nuclear reaction is not really a fire. Instead it is a dramatic melding, or blending, of atoms, called nuclear fusion.

Each atom has its own tiny center, or nucleus. Surrounding each nucleus is an electrical force field. Ordinarily, this force field repels other nuclei, pushing them away—but in a star, the nuclei meld. How come?

As the star material gathers, its inward pressure grows. The nuclei respond by zipping and zooming faster and faster, veering away from each other all the while. However, when the pressure gets high enough, the nuclei are going so fast that their speed overpowers their repulsion. Slamming into one another, they push through each other's force fields and fuse. As the nuclei meld, a smidgen of their matter vaporizes into energy. This creates a tremendous burst of furious noise, motion, and another by-product: star shine!

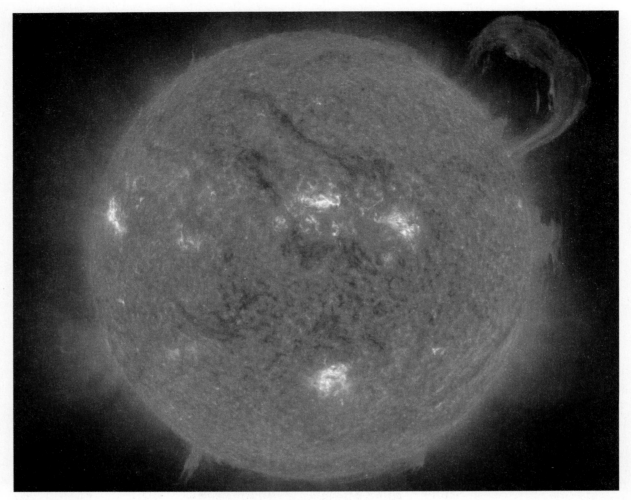

Like other stars, the Sun is a blazing ball of activity. As the brightest and hottest material rolls and swirls, darker, less-hot material sinks toward the center. The flare in the upper right is a tremendous whip of plasma lashing out into space. (False-color telescope image)

In the star's center, the gas is so energized that it has become a sort of super gas, called plasma. The hot plasma is in constant motion. It expands like hot air inside a balloon and pushes outward from the center. Meanwhile, the crushing weight of the star material continues to press inward. In goes the outer material and out goes the inner. The plasma rolls and churns like a hyper hurricane of heat, light, sound, and motion.

The star ball holds together in this perfectly balanced commotion for millions or billions of years, until the star's nuclear furnace runs out of fuel. The reaction suddenly ceases.

When that happens—look out! The end of the star is near.

Out of Fuel, Out of Time

This is a blast!

Some stars go out in a blaze of glory.

Once the nuclear reactions stop, the star's center begins to cool. The plasma slows down, its outward push growing weak. The balance is broken. The plasma collapses in on itself.

In one giant, sudden *WHOOOOOSH!*, the center of the star compresses. It caves in, growing denser and tighter than ever.

CRASH! This core material bumps—hard!—against itself.

BOOM! The material rebounds like an ocean wave slamming against a rock cliff. It pushes on the star's outer gases, which flow outward in giant surges of heat and light. As the star material rushes outward, the star grows and grows until it is a supernova, or super star. What happens next?

Possibly a black hole forms. Possibly not.

In this artist's illustration, a massive star comes to a spectacular end, its gases rebounding from the dense center and surging outward in bursts of light, heat, and motion.

In 1987 a distant star appeared as a pinpoint in the "before" picture before bursting out as the brilliant supernova in the "after" shot.

It all depends on the original mass of the star. If the star was about twenty-five to forty times the size of our Sun, then what's left of the star's center goes into a sudden collapse, called fallback. Once again, the star stuff plunges inward under its own weight. In, in, in it pulls. Tighter and tighter the material contracts, crunching in so fast and so hard that it is destroyed. Even its atoms are utterly demolished.

All the matter that once filled the center of the star shrinks down to a single, tiny point of extremely dense mass. It has no recognizable parts. But it does have one feature that makes it unique.

It has a pull of gravity so strong that it can out-pull anything else in the universe. Nothing can out-tug it. No army of tow trucks, no convoy of supersized earth haulers, no fleet of giant rocket engines. Not all of them combined.

Do you recognize this pull? It's the pull of a black hole. The star, a big, brilliant ball of light, has turned into a dark place of enormous gravitation. A black hole has formed.

Supersized Surprises

A black hole is sometimes where you least expect it.

One unexpected twist came as a black-hole discovery that scientists never dreamed of. The story begins with a mystery from nearly a hundred years ago. For decades it seemed to have nothing to do with black holes. The story ends with a big—a really big!—surprise.

Radio Mysteries

In the 1930s a telephone-company engineer named Karl Jansky was trying to track down the cause of hissing static in phone lines when he discovered something strange. Radio energy from outer space was interfering with the phone signals. After learning about Janksy's discovery, a radio engineer named Grote Reber decided to investigate.

What's the buzz?

Reber had just one little problem. To explore the radio energy, he needed a radio telescope—a telescope that could detect invisible radio energy—but there was no such thing at the time. So he invented one. He built it in his backyard in Wheaton, Illinois. Late into the night, Reber probed the sky with his new telescope, using it to locate the source of the mysterious radio energy.

Reber mapped these signals from the sky and shared his findings. Astronomers followed up with new investigations and soon began reporting more signals. Over time, with better radio telescopes, they found that some radio sources appeared as paired patches, one on either side of a tiny dot. They called these sources "radio galaxies." They also discovered other, more starlike sources—intense dots of radio energy without patches. How strange. What could these quasars (short for "quasi-stellar radio sources") be? Were they related to the radio galaxies?

In 1937 Grote Reber built this radio telescope from wood and sheet metal. His backyard wonder launched the study of invisible light energy from space.

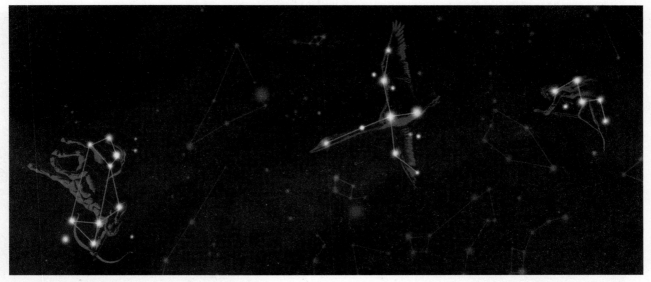

Reber found that some of the strongest radio signals from space came from the directions of familiar constellations, such as Sagittarius (the Archer), Cygnus (the Swan), and Cassiopeia (the Seated Queen). (Artist's representation)

Finally, in the early 1980s, improved images revealed a stunning new picture. The radio galaxies' patches were actually the ends of colossal streamers of energy, each one stretching hundreds of thousands of light years from the center. Something powerful had to be driving these gushing fountains of energy. And the quasars? They turned out to be far, far away, yet somehow creating radio impulses strong enough to reach Earth. No star could do this.

In fact, every quasar and radio galaxy dot turned out to be energy from the center of an entire galaxy. Astronomers found stars careening around these centers, zooming at previously unheard-of speeds in their orbits. The motion was like an accelerating ice skater pulled around her partner in a tight twirl—or like a fish caught in a superstrong whirlpool. Something extreme had to be in the middle of each of those galaxies.

In this false-color telescope image, lobes of radio energy shoot away from the center of the radio galaxy Cygnus A. Each enormous lobe is about 300,000 light years long.

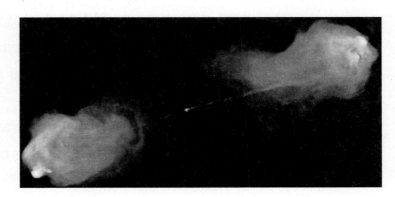

As this artist's illustration shows, matter colliding near a supermassive black hole can kick up a ruckus of energy. Such energy "footprints" help scientists in their search for black holes.

You might be able to guess what this was, but for scientists, the best answer came as a shock. In 1994 telescopic evidence confirmed the amazing cause: a *supermassive* black hole, with the mass not of one imploded star, not of two, but of millions—maybe even billions.

Imagine the excitement! Scientists had discovered a new, entirely unexpected class of black holes when they weren't even looking for one. It was like playing hide-and-seek and tripping over a whole group of people you never knew were in the game.

As it turns out, supermassive black holes are probably at the heart of almost all galaxies, including our own.

Supermassive Start-Ups

You are here

We live in the Milky Way galaxy, far out on the edge of one of its spiral arms. Our part of the galaxy is relatively calm, but in the center is a supermassive black hole, a compaction of three million Suns' worth of matter.

This black hole is pretty mellow, as supermassive black holes go. Because its X-ray signal is relatively weak, astronomers didn't find it for a long time. They still don't know how it formed.

In fact, scientists are still puzzling over how any supermassive black hole gets started. Could a single supernova lead to one? Probably not. Even the biggest stars are much too puny to do the trick. To create a supermassive black hole, a star would have to start out millions of times the mass of the Sun. Astronomers think this is unlikely, so they have come up with other ideas. One idea has to do with crashing stars.

Near the center of a galaxy, stars are crammed relatively close together. As gravity swings them around each other, high-speed crashes are inevitable. Gravity can also cause entire galaxies to swerve together in intergalactic collisions.

When the huge amount of matter in colliding stars and galaxies compacts forcefully, it might form a mid-sized, or intermediate, black hole. With enough of this going on,

Our galaxy's central black hole is calm compared to others—but it still packs a wallop! Zooming in on the center of the Milky Way, we see a white hot spot that reveals the intensely energetic activity surrounding a supermassive black hole. (False-color telescope image)

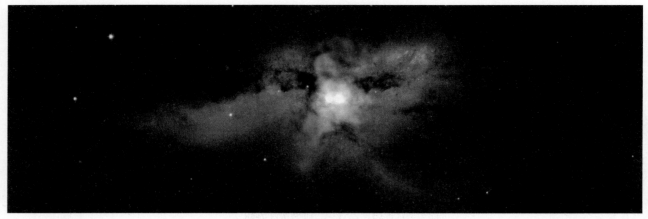

Deep in the center of the galaxy NGC 6240, two unseen supermassive black holes are merging in a slow-motion collision. The "crash" began thirty million years ago and may continue for another hundred million years or more. The collision creates a bright splash of X-ray energy, captured here in false color.

several black holes might form and then pull together, morphing into one. Nearby stars might also spiral into these growing black holes, adding to the total mass. Over time, all this piling up might lead to a supermassive black hole.

Radio galaxies, quasars, supermassive black holes—in less than one hundred years, we've made many discoveries about black holes. The theory works and the evidence is good. The conclusions seem sound.

But still . . . all of this evidence is like guessing what's inside a gift box but not being able to open it. If you could, wouldn't you want to peek inside the package and see for yourself? Wouldn't you want to visit a black hole?

Tomorrow's News

It seems that every time you turn around, astronomers are discovering something new about space. But this wasn't always the case, especially with black holes. It took several decades to go from thinking black holes could be possible to actually tracking one down.

Compare that to what's been happening more recently. Within the past decade or so, scientists confirmed that supermassive black holes exist and figured out they must be at the center of most galaxies. Astronomers found intermediate black holes, and discovered the first solo stellar-mass black holes—ones without visible partner stars. And they have tracked matter falling into a distant black hole and determined just how a black hole propels its super-energetic jets.

The fact is, you've been alive during some of the most exciting times in black-hole astronomy. Just imagine what scientists may discover by the time you're twenty!

Stay tuned . . .

Close Encounters of the Imaginary Kind

*A black hole is a destination—
for your imagination.*

Unfortunately for the curious traveler, actually visiting a black hole in the near future is downright impossible. Even the nearest black holes are too far away.

For example, one of Earth's closest black-hole "neighbors" is about 1,600 light years away. (That's about 9 quadrillion miles, or 14 quadrillion kilometers.) No spacecraft is going to get you to a black hole and back by dinnertime—even if you live to be one hundred and only want dinner on your last day.

Luckily, you can visit a black hole with your imagination. Fueled by facts, you can blast off to a black hole or two and find out what might happen once you arrive.

> ### The Closest⁺ Black Hole to Earth?
>
> If you were to aim a powerful-enough flashlight at the Moon right now, the light would reach it in a little more that a second—maybe before you got to the end of this sentence. And how long would it take for light to reach our nearest known black-hole neighbor, called V4641 Sagittarii? Fifty *billion* seconds. If you aimed your flashlight in its direction, toward the constellation Sagittarius, the light would arrive there sometime around the year 3600.
>
> ⁺Because black-hole science is booming, by the time you read this there may be a newly discovered black hole that's even closer to Earth than V4641 Sagittarii.

Are we there yet?

A Hole Variety of Places to Visit

As you take off, remember: predicting the exact details of your journey is tricky. After all, no one has ever visited a black hole, and we can't send a probe in to take a peek and send the information back to us. Not even sneak previews can escape from a black hole.

However, scientists have some best guesses about what could happen, based on what they know about gravity and black holes. A helpful rule of thumb is that close to the center of any black hole, every inch matters. Just a short distance can make an enormous difference in the strength of the black hole's gravitational effects.

The particulars of your adventure also depend on the type of black hole you visit. What size is it? Is it lumpy or smooth? Maybe it's a spinner?

Wish you were here!

Greetings from Cygnus X-1!

A spectacular view . . .

. . . of NGC 4486

Spinners, Lumpies, and Smoothies

When it comes to black holes, matter really matters. After all, if it weren't for all the matter crunched into a tiny space, an extreme gravity zone could never form. But it's not just *how much* matter in how small a space that makes a difference. *How* a star's matter collapses also affects the black hole that forms.

If the star was spinning before the collapse, then the black hole will spin, too. If the collapse is perfectly symmetric, a smooth black hole forms. On the other hand, even a slightly lopsided collapse leads to a lumpy black hole, with erratic gravitational effects. The gravity might be strong in some places and weak in others, and pull in different directions. However, a lumpy hole won't stay lumpy for long, because its own gravity will work to smooth it out.

Beyond Your Brainy Blast-Off:
Journey to a Black Hole

Suppose you were to visit a perfectly symmetric, smallish, non-spinning black hole. What would happen? Right away, you would need a new nickname—something like Stretch or the Spaghetti Kid. The pull from the black hole would force your body into a long, skinny, stringy shape. If you were going in feet first, your feet would stretch out the most. For a moment, they might look like droopy wet socks.

Not that you would notice any of this. By the time your toes could register "ouch" in your brain, your brain would not be working. This is the one time when stretching your mind might be a bad idea.

What if the black hole were lumpy? Instead of getting a nice, smooth stretch, you'd be pushed and pulled in changing directions, like human dough in a wrestling match with a pretzel maker. (The pretzel maker wins.)

Now **THAT'S** a stretch!

A kid visiting a black hole might be stretched out like spaghetti. Scientists call this phenomenon spaghettification, or the noodle effect. (Artist's representation)

**What you would see . . .
Far away from a black hole**

Approaching the event horizon

After crossing the event horizon

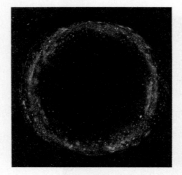

(Artist's representations)

So much for experiencing a smallish black hole; you'd have no time for sightseeing. A visit to a bigger black hole could be more interesting. It might take a while for the major effects to kick in. As you drifted in from the event horizon toward the singularity at the center, you might get a chance to look around.

What might you see? Even before you crossed the event horizon, things would start to look strange. The black hole would bend the light from all around and focus it in a miniature picture. Instead of seeing a sky full of stars, you'd see a tiny image of the black hole's surroundings, focused smack dab in the middle of the blackness overhead. Even stars on the opposite side of the black hole would be visible above you.

After you crossed the event horizon, the warped-sky image would distort even more. Now the light from everything outside the black hole would form a ring above you, like a halo overhead. Your sky would appear dark except for that bright circle—a ribbon of light that would get skinnier and skinnier as you continued to zoom inward.

You might want to tell the folks back home about this. Ah, well, too bad. Once across the event horizon, you wouldn't be able to get out any blogs or vlogs, email or phone calls, snail mail, smoke signals, messages in bottles, or signal flares to spread the news.

It would be as if you were stuck in a one-way, sightproof, soundproof bubble, sealed away from the rest of the universe. But there's no sense letting this tear you up. In a few hours, gravity will do the job instead.

Hmmm. Maybe you'd better turn that imagination of yours around and head back to Earth. That's the thing about thought experiments: they let you experience the impossible—and still get home in time for dinner.

How Far Out Is Way Out There?

Black holes are way out beyond where you are right now—much farther away than the edge of our solar system. To talk about the distance to a black hole, you'd need a huge number.

How huge? Well, in your everyday life, you probably travel only a few miles (or kilometers). At most, you might go tens of miles. Longer trips might be in the hundreds or even thousands of miles. In outer space, these distances would seem smaller than baby steps. Out there, you'd need to stock up on zeroes to describe how far it is from one place to another.

From Earth to the Sun: *millions* of miles or kilometers

From the Sun to the next closest star: *tens of trillions* of miles or kilometers

From Earth to the nearest black hole: *quadrillions* of miles or kilometers

Distance across our galaxy (Milky Way): *hundreds of quadrillions* of miles or kilometers

Distance across the observable universe (which may be much smaller than the whole universe): *sextillions* of miles or kilometers

Hundred	100
Thousand	1,000
Million	1,000,000
Billion	1,000,000,000
Trillion	1,000,000,000,000
Quadrillion	1,000,000,000,000,000
Quintillion	1,000,000,000,000,000,000
Sextillion	1,000,000,000,000,000,000,000
Septillion	1,000,000,000,000,000,000,000,000
Octillion	1,000,000,000,000,000,000,000,000,000
Nonillion	1,000,000,000,000,000,000,000,000,000,000

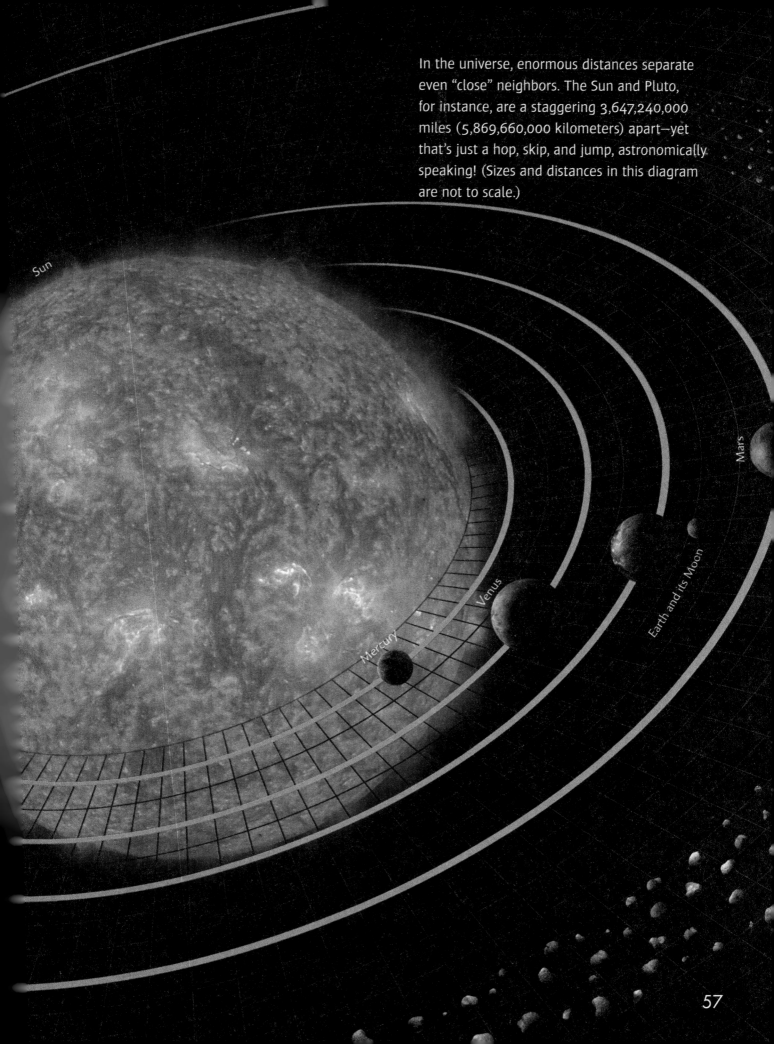

In the universe, enormous distances separate even "close" neighbors. The Sun and Pluto, for instance, are a staggering 3,647,240,000 miles (5,869,660,000 kilometers) apart—yet that's just a hop, skip, and jump, astronomically speaking! (Sizes and distances in this diagram are not to scale.)

Sun

Mercury

Venus

Earth and its Moon

Mars

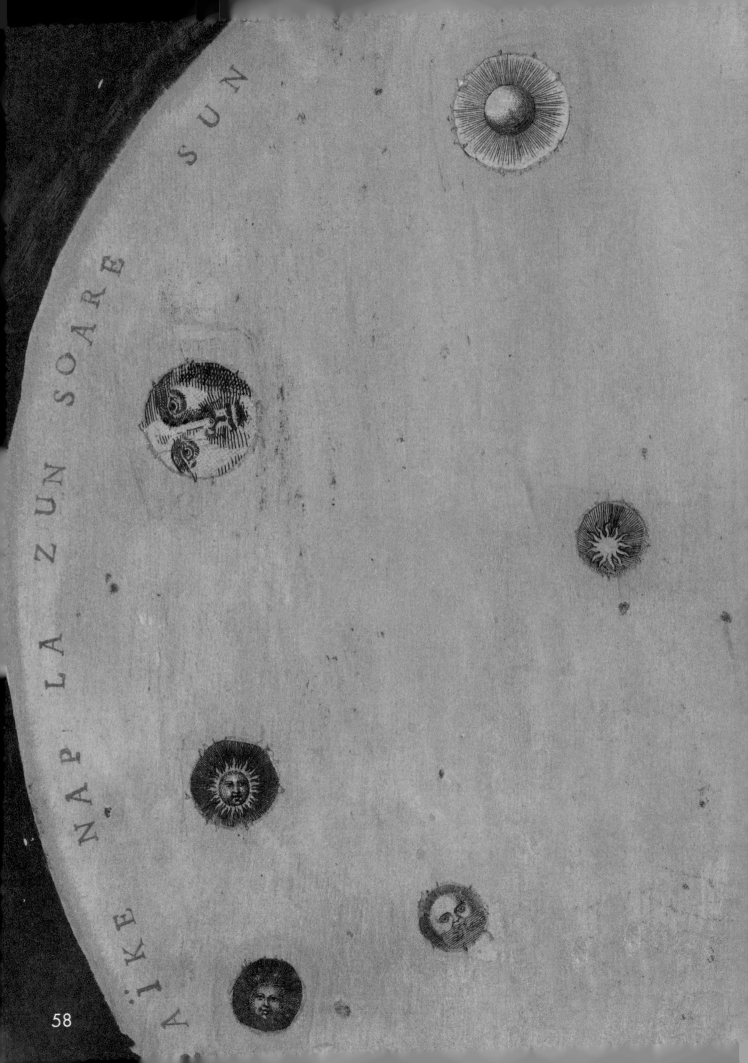

SUN

SOARE

ZUN

LA

NAP

iKE

A

the sun

by Douglas Florian

Ninety-three million miles from Earth.
Nearly a million miles in girth.
4.6 billion years old.
Core eight times as dense as gold.
Here and there a dark sunspot.
And did you know . . . the sun is hot?

SOL SOL ZON SONNE SHEMESH SAULE SOL

SOL

Great Red Spot

by Laura Purdie Salas

It's not a huge red ocean
It's not a desert form
It's twice as big as Planet Earth
And it's a great red storm

It's been around three hundred years
It's still around today
According to the weatherman
This storm is here to stay

(at least until some future day
still centuries away!)

The Great Red Spot on Jupiter is actually a giant hurricane.

the
solar system

by Douglas Florian

Each planet orbits around the sun
(A somewhat circular path).
To calculate the time it takes
Requires lots of math.

Astronomers know the planets well,
Each mountain, ring, and moon.
But none has ever gone to one,
Nor will go to one soon.

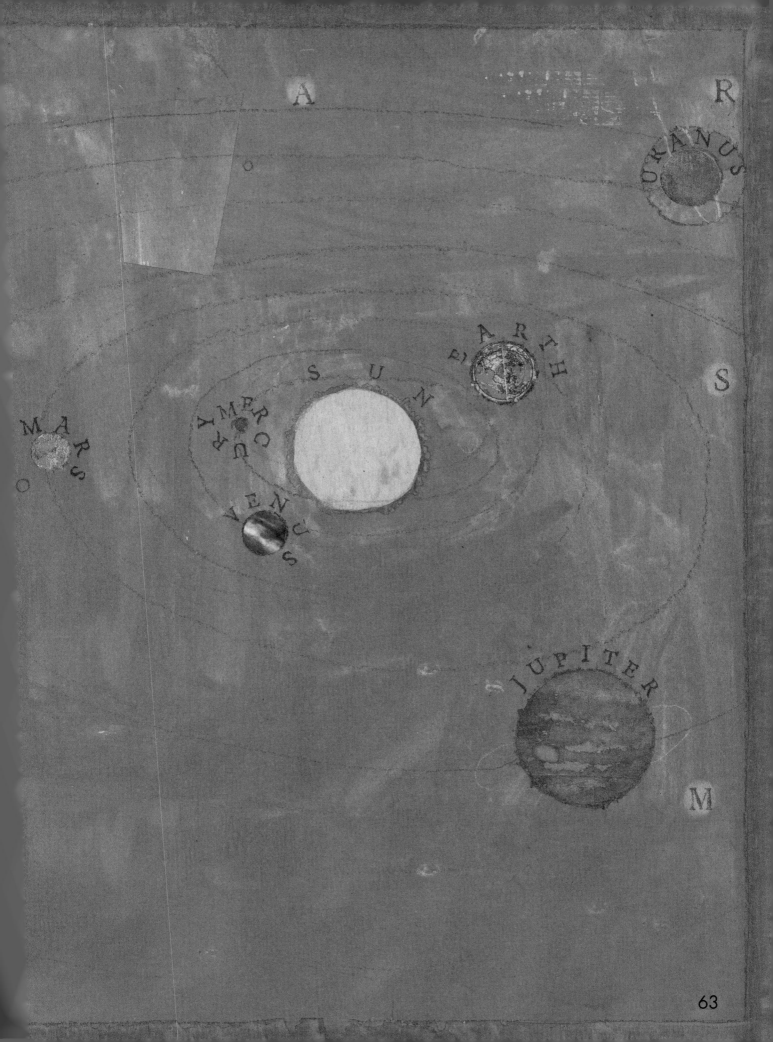

the Black hole

by Douglas Florian

Nothing's black as
A black hole
(Not black ink or lumps of coal).
Some are small
And some quite wide.
Gravity pulls
All things inside
Like a giant
Cosmic broom.
(Wish I had one in my room.)

Pedro's Journal

by Pam Conrad

August 3

The ship's roster of the *Santa María* has me down as Pedro de Salcedo, ship's boy. And the captain of this ship, who calls himself "Captain General of the Ocean Sea," has hired me not for my great love of the sea, nor for my seamanship, but because I have been taught to read and write, and he thinks it will be useful to have me along.

Last night when I boarded the *Santa María* with forty others and made ready to begin this uncertain journey to India, I saw my mother standing alone on the dock wrapped in her black shawl. She lifted her hand to wave, and I turned away quickly. I have never been away from our home. I have never been on a ship as great as this one. I dedicate this journal, this parcel of letters and drawings, to my dear mother, who has lost so much and who I pray will not lose me as well— me, her young boy whom she calls *Pedro de mi corazón*, Pedro of my heart.

We are a fleet of three ships, the *Niña* and *Pinta* with us, and this morning in the darkness, with no one watching or waving good-bye, we left the harbor at Palos and headed out for the sandbar on the Saltes River. There we waited for tide and wind and then made way for the Canary Islands. We are to be the first ships ever to run a course west to the Indies, Marco Polo's land where palaces are built of gold, where mandarins wear silk brocade and pearls are the size of ripened grapes.

A couple of the men are seasick and are already mumbling that we will never see this India our Captain General is so certain he will find. Me, I have no knowledge of maps or charts or distant journeys. I am only a ship's boy. There are three of us, and I am beginning to suspect that we will do all the work no one wants to do. But already the Captain favors me and has called upon me to write and to copy certain of his writings. I believe he is testing me and will find I am capable and write a good hand.

The Captain told me he was pleased to see my stomach is as strong as my handwriting and has encouraged me to sketch some of the things I see around me. Perhaps I am a natural seaman, although I admit that looking over the side of this creaking ship into the swelling water can fill me with terror.

September 10

Everyone seemed crazy all day. No one is doing his job well. Even the helmsman steered improperly and took us north instead of west. I thought the Captain would string up the whole crew to the mast. "What do you think you are doing?" he shouted. "Steering a ferryboat across the River of Seville?" I've seen him go into white rages and then pace his small cabin saying his Hail Marys.

We finally lost sight of land as we sailed west. Some say it will be a long time before we see it again. If at all. A couple of the men were crying, and the Captain shamed them and then promised them all sorts of riches and fame. He has said that the first man to spot land will receive a reward of 10,000 maravedis.

The men listen to him sullenly, and I see them exchange glances. They don't believe him, and after what I saw this morning, I wonder if they should. I noted that the morning's slate said we made 180 miles, and yet the Captain recorded only 144 in his official log that the men see. I believe he is trying to make the crew believe that we are closer to home than is true.

But 10,000 maravedis! Ah, think of all I could buy for my mother. Even now I can picture a beautiful dress, a rich dress that she could wear to Mass at Easter. I will keep a sharp eye. I will be the first to spot land!

October 10

This has been the worst day of all for the Captain. I am certain of this. We have doubled all previous records of days and leagues at sea, and we've gone way past the point where he originally said we would find land. There is nothing out here. Surely we are lost. And everyone is certain now as well.

This morning the men responded slowly to orders, scowling and slamming down their tools and lines. They whispered in pairs and small groups on deck and below. The air was thick with mutiny and betrayal, until finally everything came to a dead stop. The wind howled through the shrouds, and the men just stood there on deck and did not move aside when Columbus came.

"Enough," one of the men said to his face. "This is enough. Now we turn back."

The other men grumbled their assent and nodded, their fists clenched, their chests broad. And they remained motionless and unmoved while Columbus paced the deck, telling them how close he figured we must be, that land could be right over the next horizon. He told them again of the fame and fortune that would be theirs if they could only last a little longer. And they laughed at him, the cruel laughter of impatient and defeated men.

"All that aside," he added, "with the fresh easterly wind coming at us and the rising sea, we can't turn a course back to Spain right now. We would stand still in the water."

I looked up at the sails, full and straining, taking us farther and farther from Spain. What if a westerly wind never came? What if we were just blown away forever and ever?

"Let me offer you this," Columbus finally said. "Do me this favor. Stay with me this day and night, and if I don't bring you to land before day, cut off my head, and you shall return."

The men glanced at each other. Some nodded. "One day," they said. "One day, and then we turn around."

"That is all I ask," Columbus said.

Later, when I went down to the cabin with the log, the Captain's door was bolted shut, and when I knocked he didn't answer, so I sat outside the door with the heavy journal in my lap and waited.

Through the day, the day that was to have been our last day traveling westward, many things were seen floating in the water, things that stirred everyone's hopes and had the men once again scanning the horizon. We saw birds in flocks, reeds and plants floating in the water, and a small floating board, and even a stick was recovered that had iron workings on it, obviously man-made. Suddenly no one wished to turn around. There was no further word on it.

At sunset, I led the prayers and the men sang the *Salve Regina*. Then the Captain spoke to the seamen from the sterncastle, doubling the night watch and urging everyone to keep a sharp lookout. No one asked about turning back. Then the Captain added a new bonus to his reward of 10,000 maravedis. He added a silk doublet, and some of the men joked with each other. Next the Captain nodded to me, and I sang for the changing of the watch, but my words were lost in the wind that was growing brisker and in the seas that were growing heavier and sounding like breakers all about us. The men dispersed to their watches and their bunks, and the Captain paced the deck. I don't know why, but this night I stayed with him. I stayed still by the gunwale, watching over the side. Once in a while he would stand beside me, silent, looking westward, always westward.

Then, an hour before moonrise, the Captain froze beside me. "Gutierrez!" he called to one of the king's men on board, who came running. He pointed out across the water. "What do you see?"

Gutierrez peered into the west. "I don't see anything," he said. "What? What? What do you see?"

"Can't you see it?" the Captain whispered. "The light? Like a little wax candle rising and falling?"

The man at his side was quiet. I was there beside him, too, straining my own eyes to the dark horizon.

Suddenly another seaman called out across the darkness, "Land! Land!"

"He's already seen it!" I shouted. "My master's already seen it!" And the Captain laughed and tousled my hair.

"Tierra! Tierra!" It was heard all across the water from all three ships.

I am below now in the Captain's cabin writing, while in the light of the rising moon, with our sails silver in the moonlight, we three exploring ships are rolling and plunging through the swells towards land. Tomorrow our feet will touch soil, and I can assure my dear mother in the hills of Spain that no one will get much sleep on board the *Santa María* tonight!

October 12

A lush green island was there in the morning, and our three ships approached it carefully, maneuvering through breakers and a threatening barrier reef. We could see clear down to the reef in the sparkling blue waters as we sailed through. And, ah, it is truly land, truly earth, here so far from Spain. The *Santa María* led the way into the sheltered bay of the island and got a mark of only five fathoms' depth. We anchored there and barely paused to admire the breathtaking beauty. Small boats were prepared, armed, and lowered, and in these some of us went ashore. Out of respect, all waited while Christopher Columbus leaped out of the boat, his feet the first to touch this new land. (I wondered what my mother would say if she knew her son had lost the 10,000 maravedis to the Captain, who claimed it for himself.)

The Captain carried the royal banner of our king and queen, and as everyone else scrambled out of the boats and secured them in the white sand, he thrust the banner into the earth and then sank down to his knees and said a prayer of thanksgiving for our safe arrival in India. Others dropped to their knees around him. Diego was beside me, and he clapped his hand on my shoulder. I knew he was happy to be on land again. I was, too, although I have been at sea so long that even on land the ground seems to buckle and sway beneath my feet.

The Captain made a solemn ceremony and formally took possession of the land for the king and queen, naming it San Salvador. We all witnessed this, and then little by little we noticed something else—there were people stepping out from the trees, beautiful, strong, naked people, with tanned skin and straight black hair. My mother would have lowered her eyes or looked away, as I have seen her do in our home when someone dresses, but I could not take my eyes off them. Some had boldly painted their bodies or their faces, some only their eyes, some their noses. They were so beautiful and gentle. They walked towards us slowly but without fear, smiling and reaching out their hands.

The sailors watched them in wonder, and when these people came near, the crew gave them coins, little red caps, whatever they had in their pockets. Columbus himself showed one native his sword, and the native, never having seen such an instrument before, slid his fingers along the sharp edge and looked startled at his fingers that dripped blood into the sand.

Everyone was smiling and so friendly. Close up, we could see how clear and gentle their eyes were, how broad and unusual their foreheads. The Captain especially noted and said to one of his men, "See the gold in that one's nose? See how docile they are? They will be easy. We will take six back with us to Spain."

I think at this, too, my mother would have lowered her eyes.

October 16

So much has happened. There is so much to remember and record, and so much I do not think I want to tell my mother. Perhaps I will keep these letters to myself after all. The natives think that we are angels from God. They swim out to us, wave, throw themselves in the sand, hold their hands and faces to the sky, and sing and call to us. The crew loves it, and no one loves it better than Columbus. He lifts his open palms to them like a priest at Mass. I sometimes wonder if he doesn't believe these natives himself just a little bit.

They come right out to the ship in swift dugouts that sit forty men, and sometimes as they approach us the dugout tips, but in minutes they right it and begin bailing it out with hollow gourds. All day long the Indians row out to see us, bringing gifts of cotton thread, shell-tipped spears, and even brightly colored parrots that sit on our shoulders and cry out in human voices. For their trouble we give them more worthless beads, bells, and tastes of honey, which they marvel at.

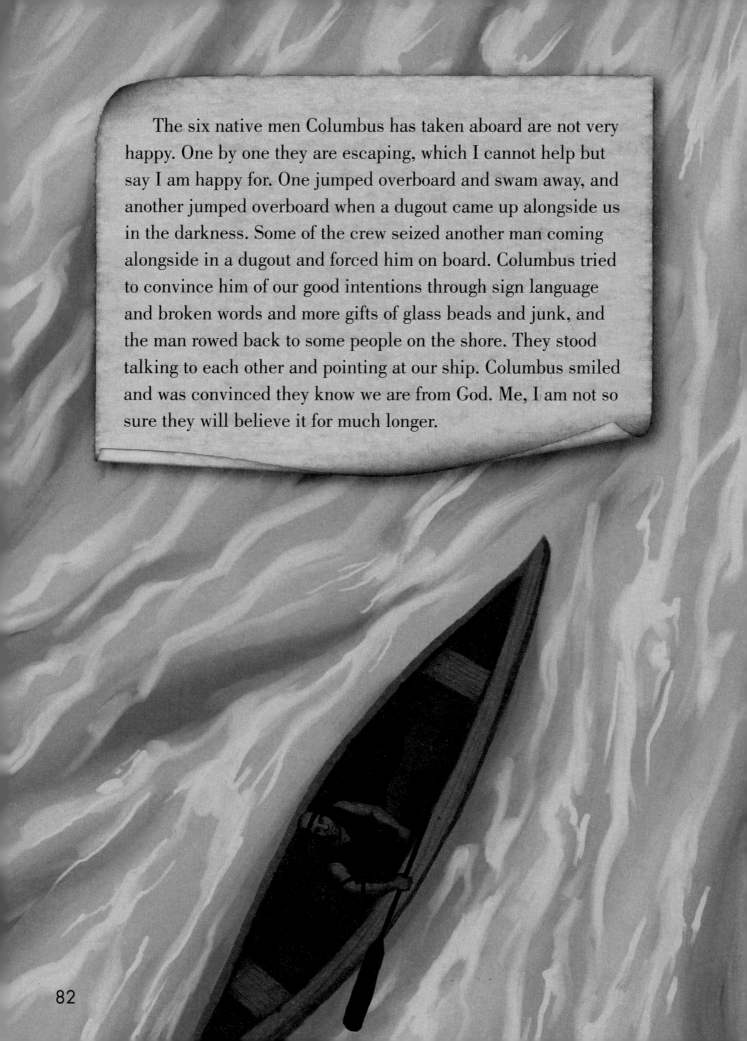

The six native men Columbus has taken aboard are not very happy. One by one they are escaping, which I cannot help but say I am happy for. One jumped overboard and swam away, and another jumped overboard when a dugout came up alongside us in the darkness. Some of the crew seized another man coming alongside in a dugout and forced him on board. Columbus tried to convince him of our good intentions through sign language and broken words and more gifts of glass beads and junk, and the man rowed back to some people on the shore. They stood talking to each other and pointing at our ship. Columbus smiled and was convinced they know we are from God. Me, I am not so sure they will believe it for much longer.

December 3

We are anchored in a quiet harbor in scattered showers. It has been raining for days without the slightest breeze or gust. Many of the men went ashore to wash their clothes and themselves in the river. Two men wandered into the jungle and returned to tell us they had come upon a village where hanging from a post was a basket with a man's head in it. I don't think I will go looking in any baskets I find.

One day I went ashore with Diego, Columbus, and a native who is working as an interpreter for us. The Captain gave Diego a bag of brass rings, glass beads, and bells and told him to see what trading he could do. Diego agreed, but I could tell he does not like to do this. A group of natives joined us, but these were not so friendly, and they had little to trade. Their eyes were distrustful, and their bodies were painted red, with bundles of feathers and darts hanging from them. When we finished our meager trade, they gathered at the stern of our small boat in the river, and one began making a speech we could not understand. The others began to shout in response. Columbus stood by looking pompous and arrogant as he waited, but the interpreter with us turned pale and began to shake. He told the Captain to go back to the *Santa María* at once, that they were planning to kill us.

I hopped right in the boat to go back, but Diego didn't move and Columbus laughed. He interrupted the village speechmaker and drew his sword from his scabbard. With a gentle smile on his face, he showed him the steel glistening in the sun, sliced clear through a leather strap the speechmaker bore around his neck, and the man's beads tumbled into the sand. Next the Captain had one of his men demonstrate his crossbow. At this the crowd of natives turned and ran into the trees. Our interpreter was still not comforted. He jumped into the boat beside me and, trembling, beckoned us to get aboard and get back to the ship, quickly.

The Captain was slow about it. He talked of how he admired the workmanship of these natives, but how cowardly they were: "They are so timid, ten of our men could frighten away thousands of them." I said nothing. The Captain expects nothing of me. I just watched silent Diego's back straining and bulging in rhythm as he helped row us back to the *Santa María*.

December 13

It is difficult to keep a journal now that we are so busy, traveling from island to island and up and down rivers and in and out of harbors. There are no longer endless empty jaunts into the western sky. But one thing has not changed. The crew continues to grumble. They are saying this is not Asia at all, that this whole trip has been a costly failure. They say they will be laughed at when we finally return home. There are no silks, no treasures, and just tiny trinkets of gold. All we will bring back are spools of rough cotton thread, a few rustic spears, and some natives who grow quieter and thinner with each day they spend on board the *Santa María*.

Columbus goes on naming everything he touches. He sees a cape of land and he says, "I christen you Cabo de la Estrella," or "Hail, Cabo del Elefante." "I name you Cabo de Cinquin," or "Isla de la Tortuga." "And you I name Puerto de San Nicolas." I am surprised he doesn't name the birds as they fly by. Every time his feet touch land he thrusts a cross into the sand and claims it for the king and queen of Spain.

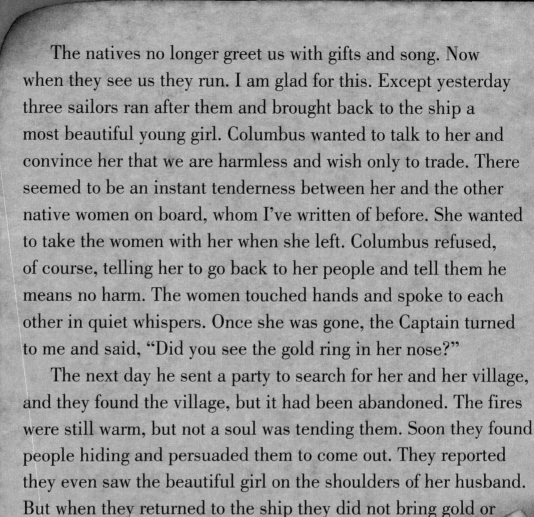

The natives no longer greet us with gifts and song. Now when they see us they run. I am glad for this. Except yesterday three sailors ran after them and brought back to the ship a most beautiful young girl. Columbus wanted to talk to her and convince her that we are harmless and wish only to trade. There seemed to be an instant tenderness between her and the other native women on board, whom I've written of before. She wanted to take the women with her when she left. Columbus refused, of course, telling her to go back to her people and tell them he means no harm. The women touched hands and spoke to each other in quiet whispers. Once she was gone, the Captain turned to me and said, "Did you see the gold ring in her nose?"

The next day he sent a party to search for her and her village, and they found the village, but it had been abandoned. The fires were still warm, but not a soul was tending them. Soon they found people hiding and persuaded them to come out. They reported they even saw the beautiful girl on the shoulders of her husband. But when they returned to the ship they did not bring gold or silks. More blessed parrots.

January 28

How wonderful this feels to be heading home. We almost made one extra stop. One of the natives on board told the Captain of an island on our way where only women live, where it is believed men come only part of the year and then are kicked out along with boy children who are old enough to leave their mothers. It was not the women the Captain was interested in, but the fact that this may be the island Marco Polo wrote about in his voyage to the Orient. And this would be the proof Columbus needs to show we did indeed make the Indies.

He even turned in this direction for two leagues, but when he saw how disappointed the men were—how even the thought of an island full of women did not distract them from their desire to go home, or their uneasiness about the leaking boats—he turned back towards our homeland, and now the ships roll before the winds, winds that grow cooler and cooler with each passing day.

February 2

   Tonight is the night of the full moon, and once again we are
traveling through a throbbing meadow of seaweed, this time at a good
speed with gentle winds pushing us along. Earlier, I was not able
to sleep for the eerie noise the seaweed brings, the soft, enchanted
swish against the hull, like a mother's hand soothing a baby's head,
so I went above and found the Captain alone on deck, lit by the
moon. His log entries these last days are concerned with the miles
we make and the direction we sail, constantly plotting and striving
to find his way back to Spain. I was uncertain at first what to do, but
finally I came up beside him. I don't think he had even looked to see
who I was, when he pointed off toward the north-northeast and said,
"I believe there are islands off in that quarter. When we come back
on our second voyage, I will make certain we visit them."

   A second voyage. Suddenly the wind was too cold for me. The
moon too bright. Below, I wrap myself tight in my blanket and
struggle to write. The inkhorn in one hand, the quill in the other, I
try to imagine myself growing to manhood on ships such as this,
and I cannot. Oh, I cannot.

SECRETS OF THE CANYON CAVE

by Gaby Triana

Canyon Kids Ranger Scott Merker propped his leather boot onto a striped boulder, hands at his hips. "Alright, everybody, this is where we begin."

Brandon Leigh and his eleven hiking companions gathered around Ranger Merker, canteens and walking sticks clattering with anticipation. He clung to every word Ranger Merker said. *I must win this scavenger hunt*, thought Brandon. He was tired of always coming in second or third place to Derrick Sweeney.

"You've already received your item list, and you have your assigned partners. Right?" Ranger Merker asked. Everyone nodded and smiled at their partners.

Brandon's gaze shifted slightly to his left, avoiding direct eye contact with Ría Sanchez. Yes, he'd been paired with a girl, but Ría was also four inches taller than him, strong, and a natural-born hiker. *This may work to our advantage*, he thought.

"You'll have from now until dusk to explore. That's two hours. Stick to the items on your list. Don't bring back extra prickly pears and expect to get extra points. Any questions?" Ranger Merker asked.

Brandon looked around and raised his hand shyly. "What if we find an item not on the list that we think might be worth something?"

Behind him, Derrick chuckled. "Like what? Golden treasure?"

Brandon wanted to turn around and glare at him, but figured it was probably what Derrick wanted. So, instead, he ignored him.

"Actually, great question, Brandon," Ranger Merker said. "If you *do* find something out of the ordinary, bring it back, and we'll calculate its point value. Okay?"

Brandon nodded, and Ranger Merker pulled out his phone and set a timer. "Okay, guys, the Southeast Utah canyons are yours. Go!"

Brandon turned to Ría, who opened her map and pointed at some squiggly lines. "Why don't we go this way? We could catch a view of these entrenched meandering rivers at Gooseneck State Park. The pictures we take could be worth lots of points."

Brandon cringed. "But it'll take too long. The other way has more stuff to see, and it's safer." Though it was true that the famous entrenched meanders were incredible geological phenomena to behold.

Ría pouted. "It's an easy hike. But fine, we'll go your way."

"Okay." Brandon would never consider a hike across pure desert *easy*, and he knew they'd find more items along his route. Still, he hoped Ría wasn't too disappointed.

They headed west underneath clear blue skies, picking up samples of snakeweed and blackbrush, and snapping photos of cottontails and prairie dogs. There was something about walking in the wide open desert air, surrounded by rock formations older than time itself, that reminded Brandon of how the explorer Francisco Vásquez de Coronado must have felt while searching for the Seven Golden Cities of Cíbola.

Immensity. Solitude. In unison with nature. In a word—incredible.

After about an hour, it was time to start heading back, but then, Brandon spotted it—a thunderhead looming on the not-too-distant horizon. "I thought it didn't rain in the canyon lands," he said.

"It does in summer!" Ría said. "But it's usually over quick. Let's find a place to hide."

Brandon couldn't believe their luck. Not that he was afraid of a thunderstorm, but it *was* getting extremely close to dusk. "Go that way." He pointed to a sandstone cliff sloping down into the canyon. "Maybe we'll find cover on the other side."

Spikes of cool air and a strong wave of humidity hit them. The burning sun disappeared behind massive dark clouds. They kept close to the cliff, close enough to examine the colored layers of rock that dominated the formation, like bottles of sand art he made when he was in preschool, only in thick sheets of burnt orange, sand, and cream.

The wind picked up in strong gusts. Soon, biting pellets of heavy rain pelted them. Ría shrieked, and Brandon urged her to move faster. A crack of thunder boomed across the canyon, but a minute after the rain began falling over the dry, rocky landscape, they slipped into an opening in the cliff.

"I'm soaked!" Ría pulled her wet clothes away from her skin.

"Me too. Lucky that we found this place," he said, his eyes adjusting to the darkness inside. As soon as they did, he stopped cold at what he saw—a long wall stretching about twenty feet in either direction. Above them, the cliff served as a ceiling, and the long opening they'd just ducked through was a wide window exposing the canyon below. In front of him, Brandon stood face-to-face with brown and red markings on the walls.

"No way," he whispered. Others had been here before them.

"Way," Ría whispered back.

Brandon stood there, mouth agape. *A cave dwelling?* He'd read about these spaces hidden inside cliffs in the Four Corners region, but was it ancient? "Ría, this might actually be an old Anasazi cliff dwelling. They were the ancient Pueblo Indians, and . . ." He looked around in wonder. "They did stuff like this."

"How can we know for sure?"

"We can't, but let's start taking pictures to show Ranger Merker when we get back."

Ría smirked. "I don't think we're going to get back anytime soon, Brandon. That storm looks pretty bad. Maybe we should call them and let them know we're stuck out here."

"Good idea." Brandon pulled out his phone and called Ranger Merker while Ría snapped photos with her phone. He let the ranger know they would get back just as soon as they could, but they were given strict instructions to stay put, since it would soon be nightfall. In the morning, officials would come get them.

Morning? Brandon wasn't thrilled at the thought of staying here overnight, with a girl no less. But at least he wasn't alone, and they *did* have backpacks filled with emergency items. Still, he never intended to be camping tonight. But Ría didn't seem to mind. Her face was alight with curiosity, as her hands traced the drawings on the walls. Simple scrawlings of stars, the moon, and a big sun shaped like a spiral. "Can you believe this? Brandon, this is amazing!"

"It is," he said, but couldn't ignore the sinking feeling in his stomach. They would *never* win the scavenger hunt now. He should've listened to Ría and gone toward Gooseneck State Park. Photos of the entrenched river would've won them the hunt for sure. Why did he have to be so cautious all the time?

"Well, I guess there's nothing to do but wait," he said, plopping onto the cold sandstone floor, crossing his legs. He watched with a heavy sigh as the driving rain pounded the rocks outside. As water pooled into small potholes and crevices, Brandon watched the sky shift from stormy gray to dark coral, then finally to deep purple and royal blue.

He'd never slept in the desert before. Would they encounter black bears, coyotes, or, worst of all—snakes? He took out his Swiss Army knife and set it next to him, just in case. Ría sat next to him, unzipped her backpack, and pulled out a water bottle and flashlight. A gust of wind whistled into the cave, chilling Brandon to the bone. The dry canyon was quickly losing its daytime heat. He yanked out his jacket from the backpack and put it on, hugging it close.

Soon, the clouds cleared away, and night unfurled over the canyon like a giant blanket of black velvet with silver glitter spilled all across it. Brandon ventured outside to admire it. Never in his life had he seen so many bright stars, shooting stars, and faint purple and yellow blotches, which he guessed might be nebulae or bands of the galaxy.

In the darkness, he vaguely detected shapes scuttling about, lizards or rodents trying to bring their meals home. In the distance, a coyote howled. Restless, Brandon returned to the cave, doing his best to imagine that he was an ancient Anasazi tribesman getting ready for a good night's sleep out of harm's way. *If they could do it, so can I.*

"Check this out," Ría's voice echoed through the dwelling. He followed her voice and the swaying of her flashlight to the opposite end, where he found her staring at a huge opening between two tall boulders, like a doorway to another world.

His gaze fell on what she saw. "What is that?" he asked, gawking at what appeared to be a kind of fence made entirely out of twigs with twine or dried plant parts binding the intersections together.

"I have no idea," she said.

"It's like a grid." Brandon noticed that this wall of interconnected sticks had notches all over it, as if someone had used a sharp object to mark it in random places.

"Maybe a trellis for growing plants?" Ría shrugged.

"Out here? Plants?" Brandon asked. What could it be? He glanced back at the cave walls. Drawings of heavenly bodies everywhere. He took out his phone, snapped a photo of the fence, and sent Ranger Merker a text message: *Look what we found. Any idea what it could be?*

"What about this?" Ría shone her flashlight at a pointed stick shooting straight up out of the floor about three feet behind the wooden grid. *How did these two objects belong together?* Brandon wondered. Suddenly, a light went on inside his head. He moved over to the pointed stick and squatted behind it. If he aligned his eye to the very top point of the stick, maybe he would see . . .

That's it!

"I got it!" he cried. "If you look past the end of this stick, it aims right at that star right there. You see it?" He pointed into the open sky.

"The North Star?" Ría asked.

"I think so!" He moved over to the grid and saw that the biggest
cut was in the shape of an asterisk, lined up perfectly with the North
Star. "They used this thing to mark Polaris." He ran his fingers
along the other cuts. "And these are all the surrounding stars that
rotate around it throughout the night. See that star, and that one
right there? Those make up the Big Dipper."

He couldn't believe it! Did Ranger Merker know about this
place? Did anyone? He couldn't wait to show his photos to everyone
when they got back.

"Totally amazing!" Ría kneeled behind the stick and stared at the
North Star through the wooden grid. "So this stick is the viewfinder,
and the grid is like . . . the binoculars." Amazing indeed. They were
truly explorers discovering new things!

They gave each other high fives and then found a corner of the cave where they would sleep for the night. They bundled up their backpacks to use as pillows and faced the dwelling opening that exposed the northern sky. As he watched the falling stars glide across the sky, Brandon could barely contain his happiness. Here he was, sleeping in the very same cave others had slept in long ago, against a backdrop of cave paintings made by the same people, with an ingenious scientific tool made by human hands over a thousand years ago! It boggled his mind.

"Good decision to come this way," Ría spoke through the darkness.

"Thanks," Brandon said. Just then, Ranger Merker's reply text came in: *Wow, looks like you found an ancient device for measuring latitudes, like the sextants of long ago, or the compasses we use today. Good job, guys! You SO win the scavenger hunt! See you in the morning.*

Brandon smiled widely. "We won," he told Ría.

"Of course we did. 'Cause we're awesome!" Her bubbly, laughing voice echoed throughout the cave. "Goodnight, Brandon."

"Goodnight." And with one last contented sigh, he closed his eyes and fell fast asleep.

CROSSROADS AMERICA™

NEW BEGINNINGS

Jamestown and the Virginia Colony
1607–1699

DANIEL ROSEN

These houses in the Colonial National Historical Park at Jamestown have been made to look like the original ones.

"*April 26th we first saw the coast of Virginia. We entered Chesapeake Bay and landed, discovering fair meadows and goodly tall trees with such fresh waters running through the woods, I was stunned at the sight.*"

—GEORGE PERCY, Jamestown colonist

Introduction

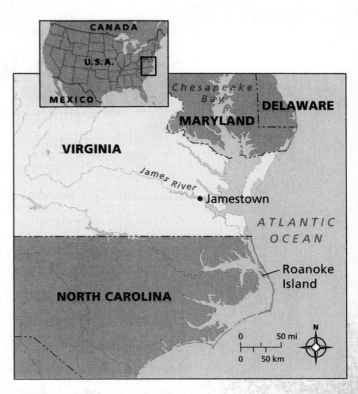

Why would people leave their homes and families to risk an ocean journey of more than 3,000 miles? Why would they give up the comforts of a settled life for the unknown dangers of a new land?

England in the late 1500s was not a pleasant place for most people. Many people were out of work. Many had lost their homes. Some saw a chance for a better life in America. They hoped to ship furs, fish, and timber back to England to make their fortune. Others believed that they would find gold and silver in America. Still others wanted to farm.

People like these were among the first small groups of English settlers who sailed to the new land. They arrived in what is now the state of Virginia. The Virginia Colony became the first permanent English settlement in America. In the earliest years of the Virginia Colony, the Virginians made some decisions that would shape the history of America.

The earliest English settlers were taking the first step on the road to building the modern United States. Many brave people followed them. This is their story.

Starting Jamestown

Virginia's story begins with a disaster. In 1587, English colonists settled on an island they called Roanoke. The island is off the coast of present-day North Carolina. The Roanoke Colony did not last. When leaders returned with supplies from England in 1590, everyone had disappeared.

The fate of the Lost Colony, as it was called, is still a mystery. This disaster stopped the English from returning to Virginia for a short time. After a while, the idea of riches won out over any fear of what might happen.

In 1606, a group of London businessmen decided they could get rich in North America. They formed a company called the Virginia Company. They asked King James I of England for a charter, or a permit, to start a colony in Virginia. The charter stated the rights, duties, and goals of the company. The king thought a colony would benefit England. He granted the charter.

Three ships left London for Virginia in December 1606. The ships carried about 100 colonists and all the things they would need. Who were these brave people? They were all men. Some of them were farmers. Others were servants. A few were skilled craftsmen. Many of them were gentlemen. At that time in England, gentlemen did not do physical labor. These men did not expect to do any work in the Virginia Colony either.

English gentlemen were not prepared for the work of building a colony.

ARRIVAL IN VIRGINIA

The English had learned something from earlier failures, but they hadn't learned enough. They sent people to the new land who had no skills or desire to work. They were not planning to clear forests and plant crops. They believed their only work would be bending over to pick up all the gold and silver on the ground. They were going to the Virginia Colony to strike it rich.

Crossing the Atlantic had left most of the travelers seasick and weak. They wondered if they had made the right choice. Then, on April 26, 1607, they first saw the coast of Virginia. The beauty of the land stunned them. Flowers were in bloom. Dense forests with wild game covered the land. The settlers saw Virginia as a land of opportunity.

For the next few weeks, the colonists explored the coast. They sailed up a river they named the James. On May 14, they chose a place for their settlement. They called it Jamestown. Both the river and the town were named in honor of England's King James I.

These are copies of two of the three Jamestown ships, the *Susan Constant* (left) and the *Godspeed* (right).

THE COLONISTS AND THE NATIVE AMERICANS

The Native Americans who lived in the area were the Powhatan (pow-uh-TAN). They were a tall, dignified people. They farmed, fished, and hunted. They had a powerful chief, also called Powhatan. He led some nine thousand people. The Powhatan men were warriors. They thought of war as a kind of deadly sport. Men went to war to show their courage. Raids on enemy villages were common. So, the settlers' first task was to build a log fort.

Watercolor painting of Powhatan warrior with spear

Relations between the Indians and the settlers were always uneasy. To the Powhatan, the colonists were invaders. The English thought they were bringing civilization to the Indians. They believed that the English way of life was the best way.

Yet, the settlers needed Powhatan help. They traded with the Indians for food. The Powhatan were glad to trade for metal tools and guns. They didn't know how to make such things. But they had little food to trade. They grew only enough food to last into early spring. The settlers' demands put the tribe at risk. If they gave the settlers too much food, they themselves could starve. The differences between the Indians and colonists would cause trouble between the two groups.

Voices from America

"In our great need, the Indians brought us corn when we rather expected they would destroy us."

—JOHN SMITH, leader of the Virginia Colony

THE FIRST MONTHS

Soon, problems developed. The place the colonists chose for their settlement proved to be a mistake. They had chosen land that stuck out into the river. They thought that this made good sense. The deep water let the colonists tie their ships up close to land. But the land was marshy. The soil was poor. Salt water backed up from the ocean and got into the drinking water. Mosquitoes thrived in the marshy land. The mosquitoes spread malaria. The disease killed many settlers.

Many colonists became ill from drinking the bad water. The few crops the men had planted were not yet ripe. They were low on supplies. The settlers grew weak from lack of food. They were often unable to hunt or fish because of the danger of attack by the Native Americans. Life in Jamestown did not get off to a good start. These early months were hard.

| Settlers gathering logs to build a fence around the fort.

A Leader Saves the Colony

All through that first summer, people died. By September, more than half the settlers were dead. The leaders argued among themselves. No one could decide what to do. Would Jamestown suffer the same fate as the Lost Colony? The settlers needed a leader, or they would all die.

| Captain John Smith

At last, one man took charge. His name was Captain John Smith. Smith was 27 years old when he arrived in Jamestown. As a soldier, he already had lived through enough adventures for a man twice his age. He knew how to survive in the wilderness. He knew that the settlers had to work and farm, not search for gold.

Smith gave orders for each man to work on building the fort and gathering food. When the gentlemen reminded Smith of their rank, Smith had a simple answer: "He who will not work, will not eat." The gentlemen went to work. Smith helped the settlers survive.

| Powhatan village

"Princess Pocahontas risked the beating out of her own brains to save mine. Not only that, but she so won over her father that I was safely conducted to Jamestown."

—JOHN SMITH

Pocahontas pleading with her father to save John Smith's life

JOHN SMITH AND POCAHONTAS

In December 1607, Smith almost died when the Indians captured him. They took him to the chief. Smith later wrote a book about his experiences. When the warriors picked up their clubs and rocks, he was certain he was about to die. According to Smith, just before they came at him, Pocahontas, Powhatan's 13-year-old daughter, rushed out. She laid her head across Smith's body.

In Smith's account, the chief was moved by his daughter's actions. Instead of killing him, they adopted Smith into the tribe. He returned to Jamestown with not only his life. He had also won the friendship of the chief.

Pocahontas did more than save John Smith's life. Over the next few years, she helped save the colony. She brought food to the colonists. She also helped the newcomers trade for goods with her people. She warned the settlers about raids the Powhatan planned against them. They were able to prepare themselves for battle because of her early warnings.

A DEADLY TIME

The Powhatan released Smith in January 1608. When he returned to Jamestown, he found a group of cold and hungry settlers. Smith was a great leader, but the colony still faced many challenges.

Remarkably, on the same day he returned, a ship from England sailed up the river. It carried about 100 new settlers, along with food and supplies. The colony's bad luck continued, however. A few days later, a fire broke out in the village, destroying most of it.

Soon after new settlers arrived, a fire burned houses inside the walls of the fort.

While the settlers rebuilt their village, Smith went back to the Powhatan to trade for food. The Native Americans and the settlers also exchanged hostages as a way of keeping the peace. Still, the weakened settlers continued to die. By spring, only 38 were left. Most had died of starvation or illness.

MEET | Tom Savage

Tom Savage was a 13-year-old orphan in England. In 1608, he talked his way onto Captain Newport's ship that was sailing for Jamestown. The captain liked the boy. He took him on as an indentured servant. That meant Tom would have to work for Newport for seven years to pay for his passage to America.

In Jamestown, Tom expected to work as a field hand for Newport. Then, Captain Newport and John Smith discovered that Native American tribes sometimes traded children. So, the colonists exchanged Tom for an Indian boy named Namontack.

Tom lived with the Powhatan for three years. He learned their language and their customs. Tom became a spy for the colonists. He told them when the Powhatan planned attacks. As a reward, Newport freed Tom from his indenture.

TROUBLE AHEAD

In the fall of 1608, another ship arrived with more settlers, including the first two women. Bad luck continued. Rats had eaten most of the ship's supplies for the settlers. Smith organized fishing and hunting parties. He made sure everyone worked hard to get food. As a result, very few settlers died that winter.

In 1609, John Smith was badly hurt. By accident, his bag carrying his gunpowder exploded. He sailed back to England to get treatment for his injuries. Before leaving Jamestown, Smith looked over the storehouses. He was pleased to see that the colony had enough food to get through the winter.

The future of Jamestown looked brighter. There were now about 500 colonists. Among the new colonists was a woman named Anne Burras. She married settler John Laydon. It was the first wedding in Jamestown.

Smith planned to return to Jamestown. Although he returned to America, he never made it back to Jamestown. However, he wrote a book that told of life there. His book inspired many people to come to North America. Smith thought he had left a colony that would have no trouble surviving.

More women arrived in Jamestown after 1609.

THE STARVING TIME

When John Smith left Jamestown, there were 500 settlers. By the spring of 1610, only 60 were still alive. What could have happened in such a short time? How did the settlers die?

The Powhatan had become more and more angry with the settlers for taking their land. With Smith gone, they decided to try to wipe out the colony. They would starve the colonists.

They killed off the wild game around Jamestown that the colonists hunted for meat. Then they surrounded the village. The colonists could not leave to hunt or fish. Quickly they went through their storehouse of food. Then they ate their cattle and goats. Next they ate their dogs and finally rats and mice.

The colonists starved and died through that long, terrible winter. By spring, the few who were left were ready to leave the colony. Jamestown seemed to be finished at last. The colonists called the winter of 1609–1610 the Starving Time.

A New Beginning

In the late spring of 1610, a single ship sailed into Jamestown harbor. The passengers and crew were shocked by what they found. The few remaining settlers were eager to leave. They packed up what little of value they had and climbed aboard the ship, ready to return to England. Was this finally the end of Jamestown?

As the ship began to sail down the James River, three more English ships appeared. They were bringing more colonists, some soldiers, and food and supplies to the colony. The new governor, Lord Thomas De la Warr (for whom the state of Delaware is named), was aboard. He ordered the fleeing colonists to turn around and go back to Jamestown.

De la Warr took charge of the colony. He set out to change the way the colony was run. He put the new settlers to work immediately. The colony now tried harder to get along with the Powhatan. For several years the two groups were able to live together in peace. Jamestown would survive. But how would the settlers earn money?

Royal governor Lord De la Warr arrives in Jamestown.

BROWN GOLD

By now everyone knew that no gold or silver was to be found in the Virginia Colony. The colonists needed to find some other way to make money. One of the settlers, John Rolfe, had an idea. Smoking tobacco had become popular in Europe.

Tobacco grew wild in the Virginia Colony, but it tasted harsh and bitter. Rolfe began experimenting with tobacco plants. After many tries, Rolfe grew a plant that had a sweet taste. In 1614, he sent the first of the new tobacco to England. The people loved it. Jamestown had a future! By 1616, the colony was sending more than 2,000 pounds of tobacco to Europe.

Everyone rushed to grow tobacco. Many colonists stopped growing food crops to plant all their land with tobacco. They even planted it along the streets of the town. The governor insisted that every colonist grow at least some corn. Otherwise, the colony would go hungry. At least the colonists had a way to make money. For the first time they were working hard. Maybe the colony would make it after all.

Tobacco farming made the colony profitable.

JOHN ROLFE AND POCAHONTAS

Because of tobacco, John Rolfe became one of the most famous colonists. He is also remembered for another reason. He married Pocahontas, daughter of the Powhatan chief.

One day, Pocahontas was visiting friends when the settlers kidnapped her. The Powhatan and the settlers were not getting along. The colonists hoped to trade Pocahontas for peace with the Indians.

Chief Powhatan did not reply to this offer for three months. During this time, the colonists treated Pocahontas well. She learned English. She learned the manners of a "proper" Englishwoman. She became a Christian and was given the name of Rebecca. She felt at home with the settlers.

Pocahontas met the tobacco planter, John Rolfe. The two fell in love. Rolfe wrote a letter to the governor asking to marry her. Pocahontas also asked Powhatan. Both men agreed. The wedding was held in April 1614, in the church in Jamestown. Pocahontas's father did not come. But her uncle, an important chief, came for the ceremony.

The wedding of Pocahontas and John Rolfe

Voices from America

"It is Pocahontas, to whom my hearty and best thoughts are, and have been a long time. . . ."

—JOHN ROLFE, in a letter to the governor

THE PEACE OF POCAHONTAS

Rolfe and Pocahontas had a baby boy, Thomas. The young family went to England on a visit. They went to attract new settlers to the colony and to help tobacco sales. People became very interested in Pocahontas. She was known as Lady Rebecca. King James I and Queen Anne received her. She had her portrait painted. Pocahontas became popular in London society.

While in England, Pocahontas became ill. Just as the young family was ready to return to Virginia in 1617, Pocahontas died. She was only 22. John Rolfe, alone and sad, returned to Virginia. Thomas stayed with relatives in England and went to school there. When he was a young man, Thomas returned to Virginia.

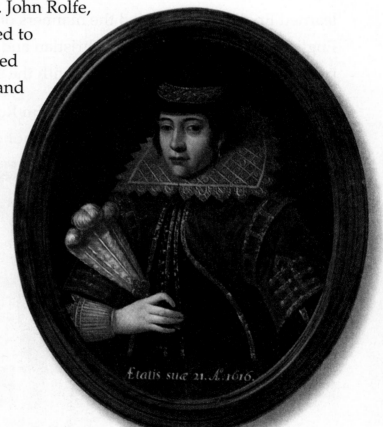

Pocahontas dressed in English clothes

MASSACRE

Pocahontas and John Rolfe's marriage helped keep the peace for a while. Chief Powhatan made sure of that. Then in 1618, Powhatan died. His brother became the new leader of the Powhatan people. This new leader did not like or trust the English. He planned to get rid of the settlers once and for all. He took his time to prepare. He wanted to take the settlers by surprise.

After years of peace, the colonists felt safe. They stopped carrying guns everywhere. They traded with the Indians. Peace seemed to rule the day. Then in March 1622, the Powhatan chief led a group to Jamestown. They came to trade furs and corn for English goods. At least that is what the settlers thought. Suddenly, the Native Americans turned on the settlers. They killed about 350 colonists, roughly a third of the total. One of them was John Rolfe.

| The Powhatan attack

THE NATIVE AMERICANS ARE DEFEATED

The massacre of 1622 was another setback for Jamestown. It also marked the beginning of the end for the Native Americans. The colonists armed themselves. They started regular attacks on the Indians. They destroyed crops and burned Indian villages. Native Americans' arrows were no match for English guns, and many Indians were killed. They learned that the colonists could not be beaten.

After the massacre, the colonists began to attack the Indians.

Voices from America

"We may now by right of war and law of nations invade the country and destroy them who sought to destroy us."

—EDWARD WATERHOUSE, a settler

The Virginia Colony Grows

Few people in England wanted to move to the Virginia Colony in its very early years. They had heard of the sickness, the unfriendly Indians, and the starvation. However, as time passed, they saw how successful growing tobacco was. Settlers were becoming rich. Also, the danger of Indian attack was fading.

Leaders of the colony wanted more settlers. So, they offered 50 acres of land in the colony to anyone who would pay for the trip. And for each additional person you brought, you got another 50 acres. A person with some money could quickly put together a large piece of land. For many, this was a great opportunity.

The Virginia Colony began to attract more settlers. In 1619, more than 1,000 settlers came to Virginia. Another 3,500 people arrived over the next three years. Many were hardworking people. Some were beggars. Others were teenaged orphans. All of them hoped to make a better life for themselves.

A Map and a Dream

by Karen O'Donnell Taylor

Maps are more
than tiny lines
intersecting
lace designs . . .
More than names
and colored dots,
rivers, mountains,
tourist spots.
Maps are keys
to secret places
vast new worlds
and unknown faces.
I can trace each
graceful line . . .
Close my eyes
and in my mind
I can travel
anywhere . . .
A map, a dream
can take me there!

Learning the World

by Kristine O'Connell George

I'm memorizing oceans,
tracing rivers,
learning mountain ranges.
I'm memorizing capitals,
tracing countries,
learning crops and industries.

I'm smoothing out this map,
rolling it into a tube,
peering through one end,
wishing it were a telescope,
wishing I could see past my street,
wishing I could see
the whole world
spread beneath my feet.

Cliff Dwelling

by John Gould Fletcher

The canyon is heaped with stones and undergrowth.
The heat that falls from the sky
Beats at the walls, slides and reverberates
Down in a wave of gray dust and white fire,
Choking the breath and eyes.

The ponies straggle and scramble
Half way up, along the canyon wall.
Their listless riders seldom lift
A weary hand to guide their feet.
Stones are loosened and clatter
Down to the sun-baked depths.

Nothing ever has lived here;
Nothing could ever live here:
Two hawks, screaming and wheeling,
Rouse a few eyes to look aloft.

Boldly poised in a shelf of the stone,
Tiny walls look down at us,
Towers with little square windows.

When we plod up to them,
And dismounting fasten our horses,
Suddenly a blue-gray flock of doves
Bursts in a flutter of wings from the shadows.

Shards of pots and shreds of straw,
Empty brush-roofed rooms in darkness:
And the sound of water tinkling—
A clock that ticks the centuries off in silence.

122

Christopher Columbus

by J. Patrick Lewis

Spain dispatched three ships
Across the Atlantic on a
Navigator's hopeless dream of
Traveling westward to Asia.
All dreams end in surprise.

Morning, October 12, 1492:
A*hoy!* In the Bahamas, he had
Reached the wilder shores of
Inhabitation, lost in the future,
Anchored at the far end of destiny.

Latitude Longitude Dreams

by Drew Lamm and James Hildreth

Magellan moved via stars
Steered his ship by celestial rays.
Columbus sailed on over the edge
Discovering lands and waterways.

They traversed their dreams, set their course
Voyaging over oceans and seas.
Etching earth with invisible designs
Crossing rivers, ice, and trees.

These lines that slide from pole to pole
Wrapping around the watery girth
Coordinate all of us on this globe
Our home, our ship, our planet earth.

Early Explorers

by Marilyn Singer

No place on earth
     is ever undiscovered
Even in Antarctica
     where whole mountains are hidden
      under ice
penguins already laid shambling tracks
     in the snow
     before we traveled there
The hottest desert
     the deepest jungle
     where none of us have ever been
all have been crossed
     and crossed again
     by wings whirring or silent
      feet furred or scaled
       hoofed or bare
By adventurers we will never know
     explorers who will never tell us
     what wonders they have seen